HOMEMADE MUSICAL INSTRUMENTS

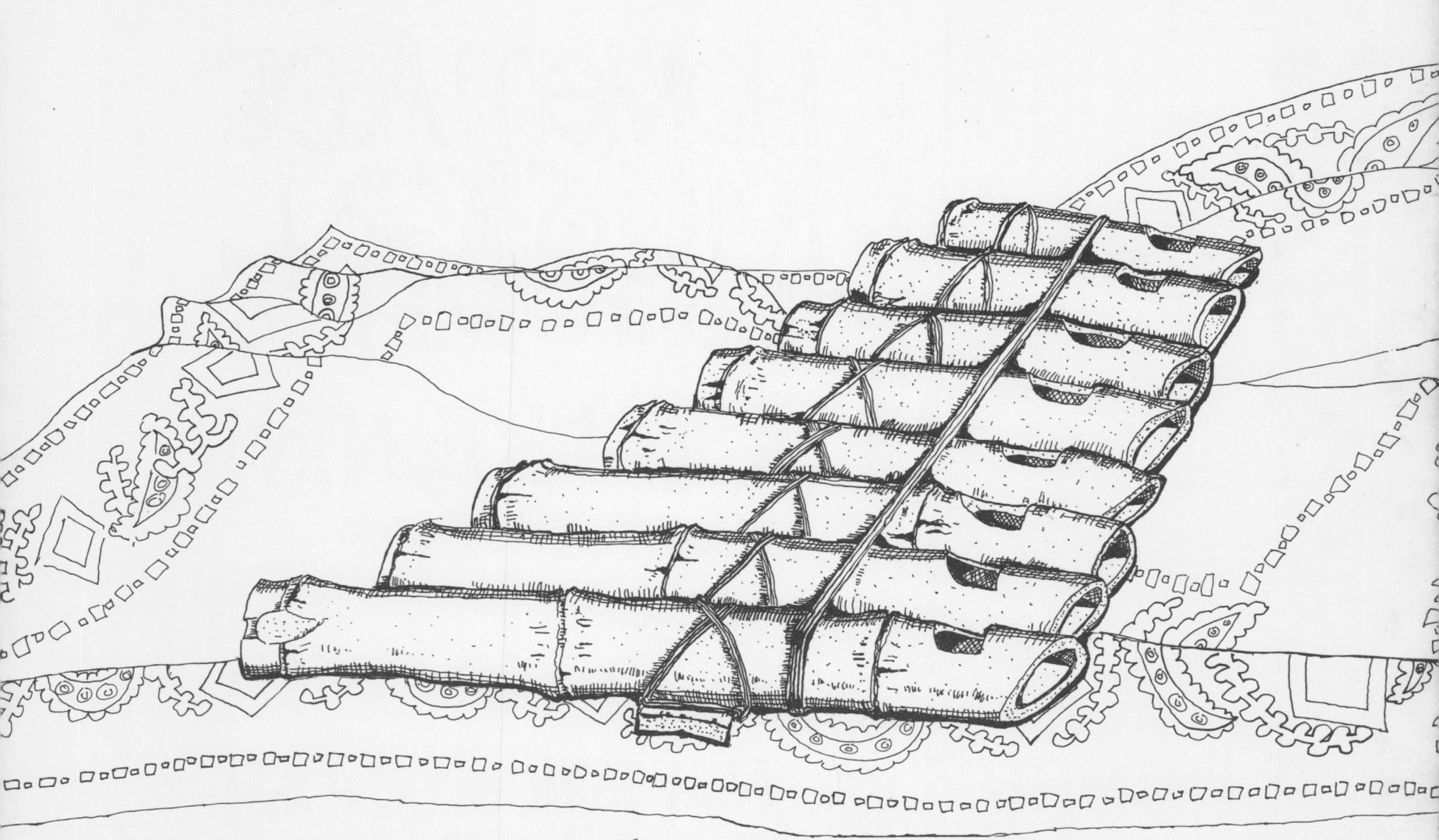

On summer nights, when I was a child in Alabama, three old black men used to go from door to door. One played a fiddle. The other played a bass. And the third made and played these pipes. He played the most beautiful Delta blues I have ever heard. There are instructions in this book for making pipes like his. But nobody can teach anyone to play the blues the way he played them.

HOMEMADE MUSICAL INSTRUMENTS

by TOM KEYNTON

DRAKE PUBLISHERS, INC. NEW YORK & LONDON

Published in 1975 by
Drake Publishers, Inc.
381 Park Avenue South
New York, New York 10016

Library of Congress Cataloging in Publication Data

Keynton, Tom
  HOMEMADE MUSICAL INSTRUMENTS

  1. Musical Instruments-Construction. I. Title
ML460. K48   781.9'1   75-10890
ISBN 0-8473-1128-7

                    0

Printed in the United States of America

DEDICATION

The gift is small but love is all

FOR C.R.A.

INTRODUCTION

I have written a book about musical instruments. To follow the title, it is a book about homemade musical instruments and the ones I have chosen I have done so because of their appearance in or their influence of the almost all-encompassing American musical heritage. Most of the instruments, though not all, are of a folk nature and many represent a naïve tradition in instrument-building and are, in that sense, homemade.

The moment anyone writes something for print he has, for one reader or another, either said too much or not enough. I confess that my own effort has been to say a little about a lot. There are a great many authors more knowledgable than this one who have written much on specific areas of musical instrument making. Many have been of value to me and a source guide at the back of this book can direct the reader on to them.

There are several plans and diagrams in this book and many notes on construction that will be of use to the amateur musical instrument maker and there are also ramblings and perambulations and incidental bits of information about musical instruments, their making and their makers. This is a book that is intended to amuse as well as instruct. If it does some of each my work is rewarded.

I have drawn upon my own experiences and from my own background as well as upon friends' and authorities'. It is my hope that this is a book of musical instruments not only for the ears but also for the eyes.

CONTENTS

Banjos 1

The Musical Bow 6

The Pluriare 12

Harp 14

Zithers & Fiddles 15

The Dulcimer 24

Horns 32

Conch Shell Trumpets 44

Clay Trumpets 46

Whistles & Whistling Jars 48

Pan's Pipes 56

Recorders 58
Fifes 62
Ocarinas & Mouthorgans 64
Bull roarer 67
Benjamin Franklin's Armonica 68
Drums 78
Bodhram 80
Steel Drums 84
Sansa, Thumb-piano 88
Nail violin & Nunut 94
Kani Niu 96
Puili 97
Ipu 98

Uli uli 99

Scrapers, Maracas, Gourds &
      Harry Partch 100

Una-Fon 105

Tap shoes 106

Acknowledgments 109

Source Guide 111

HOMEMADE MUSICAL instruMENts

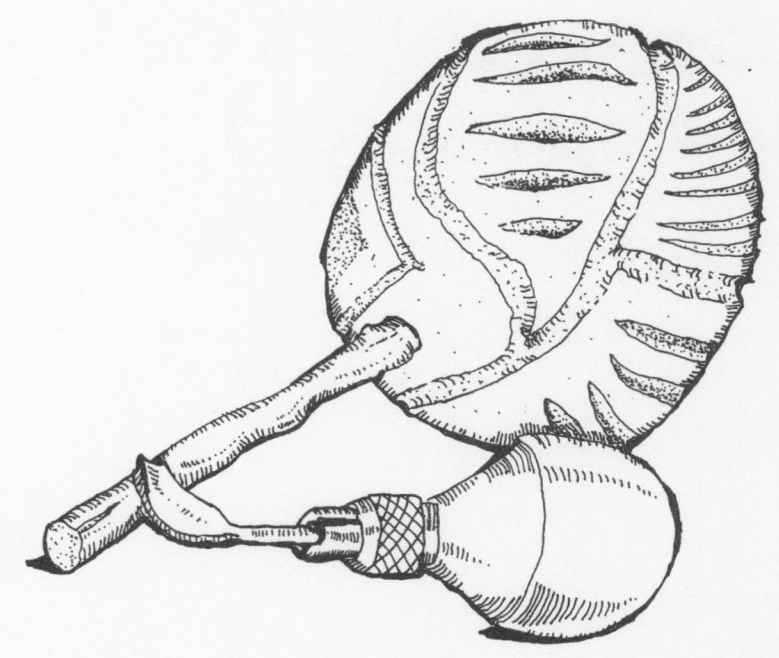

banjo, n. (pl. -os, -oes,). Stringed music
al instrument with guitar neck &
head, tambourine body, played with
fingers. Hence banjõ IST (3) n. [negro
corruption of earlier bandore ult. f. Gk.
pandoura]

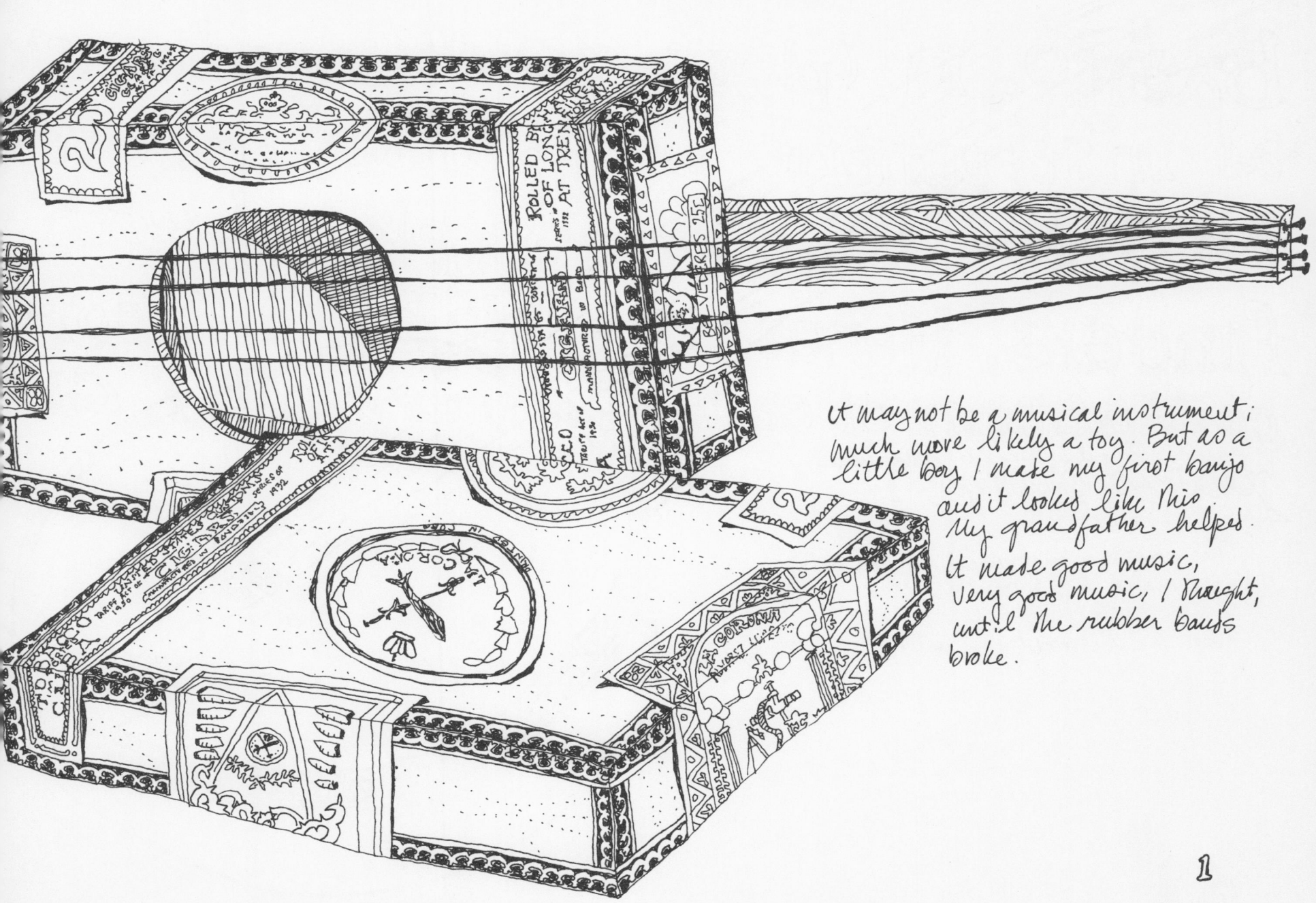

It may not be a musical instrument; much more likely a toy. But as a little boy I made my first banjo and it looked like this. My grandfather helped.

It made good music, very good music, I thought, until the rubber bands broke.

1

The five-string banjo is the true
American folk musical instrument.
Brought to America in the memories
of black slaves who, instead of the
gourds they had used in their homelands,
employed a drum-like resonator.

This particular instrument, without frets,
was made before the Civil War.

From the Metropolitan Museum of Art, New York.

2

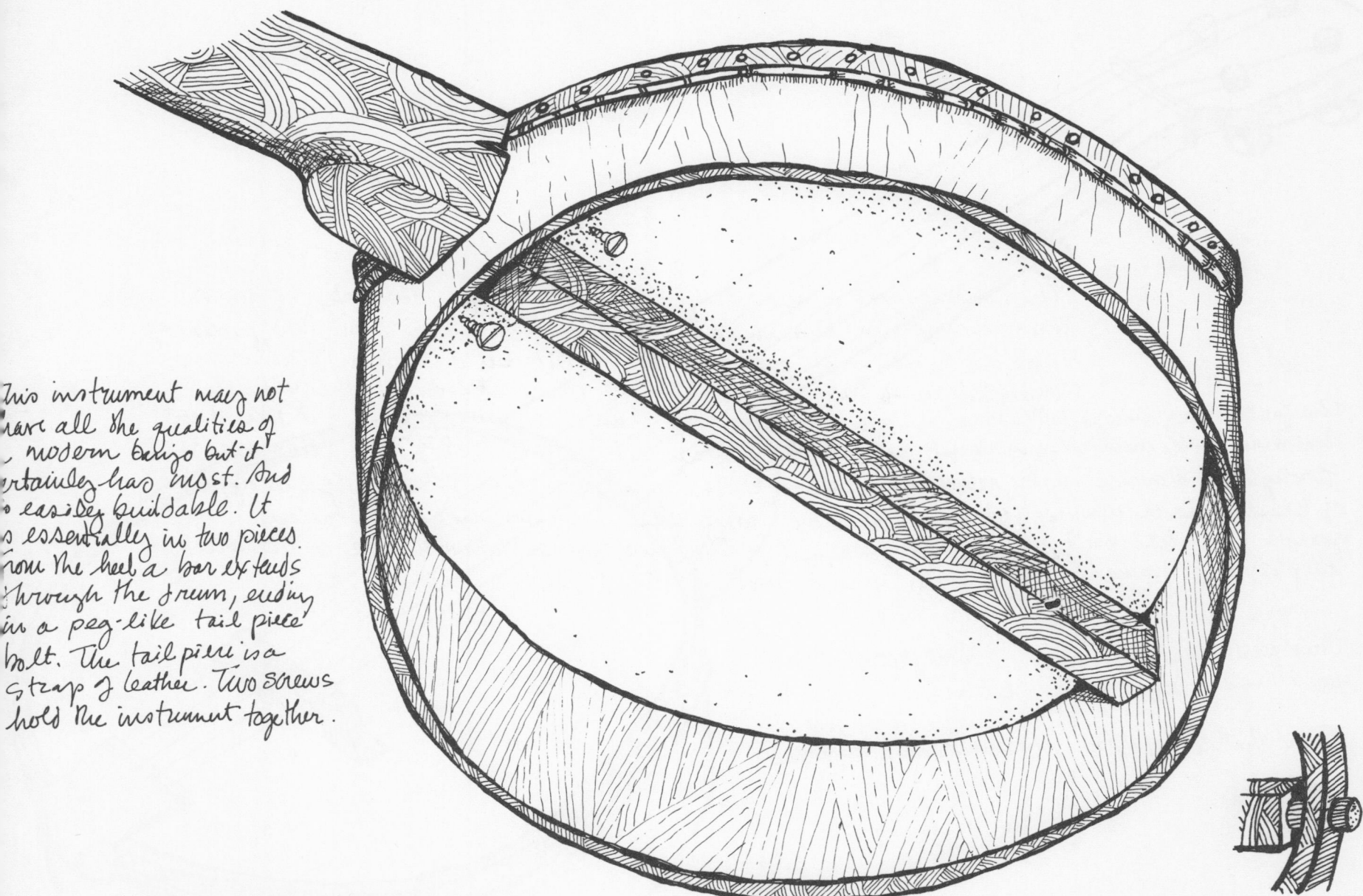

This instrument may not have all the qualities of a modern banjo but it certainly has most. And is easily buildable. It is essentially in two pieces. From the heel a bar extends through the drum, ending in a peg-like tail piece bolt. The tail piece is a strap of leather. Two screws hold the instrument together.

3

This instrument is an example of what I hope this book is about. This instrument is homemade. The hoop is made from two pieces of walnut book shelf found on the street by its maker, Guiliano, a musician and instrument builder who works on Wall Street. The head is a small drum-top from a music store and is the most expensive part of the instrument. It cost $3.75. This banjo is well made, has a fine tone, and has strong visual appeal as well. No plans were used. There were no detailed instructions or a kit. The instrument was made with care, a good eye and a well-trained ear.

4

Guilliano's homemade banjo.

5

bow[1] (bō), n. Curve; rainbow; weapon for shooting arrows (*bend, draw, the* b.; *two strings to one's* b., *more resources than one; draw the long* b., *exaggerate*); = SADDLE-b.; rod with stretched horse-hair for playing violin &c., *single passage of this across strings*; slipknot with single or double loop, ribbon &c. so tied; bb., *b-compass(es)*, compass with jointed legs; *b-head*, Greenland whale; *b-legged*, bandy; *b-saw*, narrow saw stretched like bow-string on wooden frame; *bowshot*, distance to which b. can send arrow [OE *boga*; com. Teut. cf. G *bogen* f. bug-st. of O Teut. *beugan* bend]

6

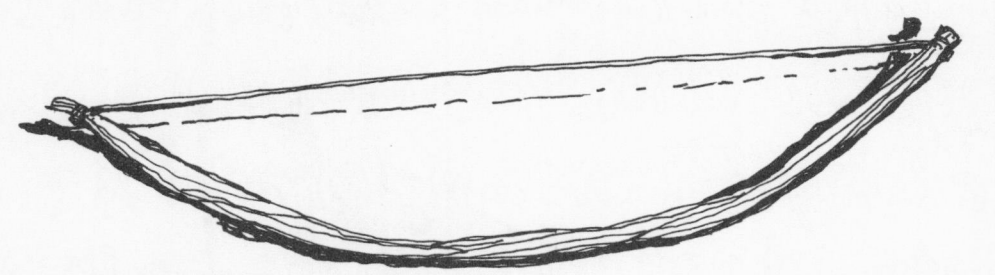

The bow may be one of the earliest forms of musical instruments. And it is possible that it is the ancestor of all stringed instruments. Because of its simplicity, it's hard to say that it developed in just one place and spread, or in one particular form and evolved. Evidences of the bow are found in almost all parts of the Old world and it is believed to have existed among the ancient cultures of Mexico and California. It is probable that the earliest musical bows were hunters' bows, that a hunter discovered that the sound of an arrow passing his bow could be reproduced by plucking the bow with his finger. The sound could be enriched by placing one end of the bow over a hole in the ground. When one end of the bow is held against the face, right at the cheek, and the bow-string is plucked, the same thing happens. But now there is control over the resonator opening. A gourd, in some places, was added as a resonator and in Africa today that is the most common form of the musical bow though tin cans are often used as resonators now. Interesting, though possibly entirely incidental; the gourd is one of man's earliest packaging devices, it was used as a bottle, a vessel, a carrying device, a drinking cup, a bowl and to imagine its being substituted with a tin can resonator on African musical bows tends to boggle the mind. At least mine.

The sound of the mouth bow resembles the sound made by the jews harp (more properly, the JAWS HARP from which the more common name is derived). The mouth bow's sound, however, is a bit sweeter and more mellow. Anyone familiar with the work of Buffy Sainte-Marie has already become aware of the renewed interest in the mouth bow. On the next few pages are notes that may be helpful for someone making a musical bow.

To make a mouth bow all you really need to do is bend a branch and tie it off with some string or wire. But if you play one often enough or just feel like making a better one, whittle out a hole and drive in a guitar peg. Of course this will be the end that you hold down and not the one you press against your cheek.

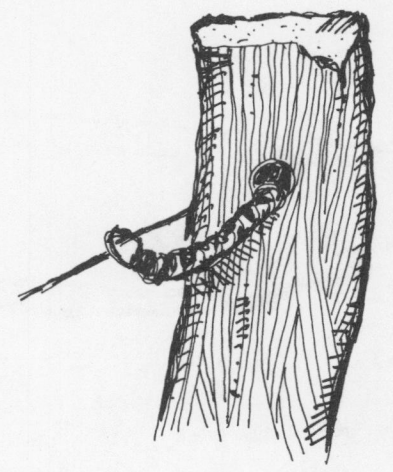

Depending on the sort of sound you like best you can use a steel or nylon guitar string.

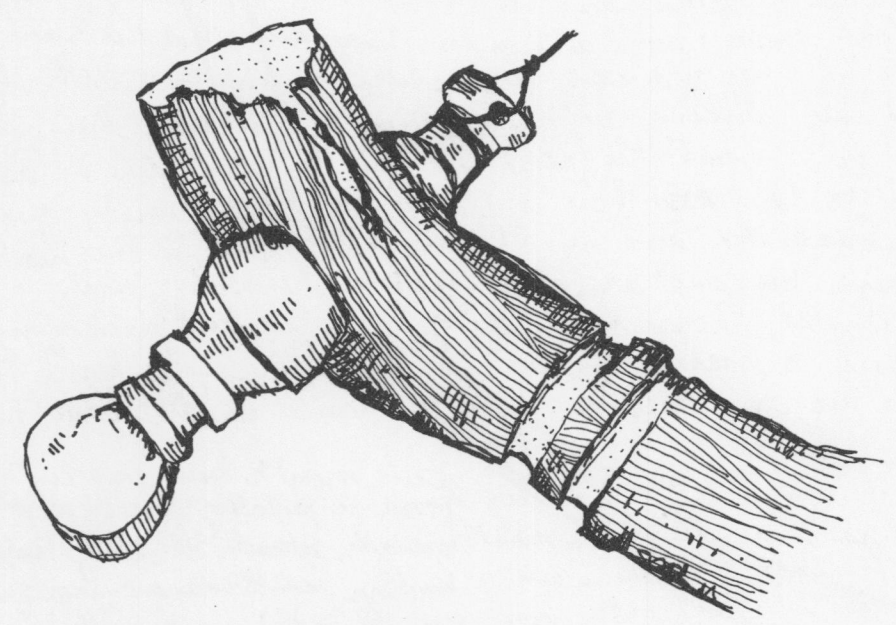

The little notched-out decoration is just that. It does give the bow some visual interest. Beads, feathers, ribbons, jangles, or bells can also be used.

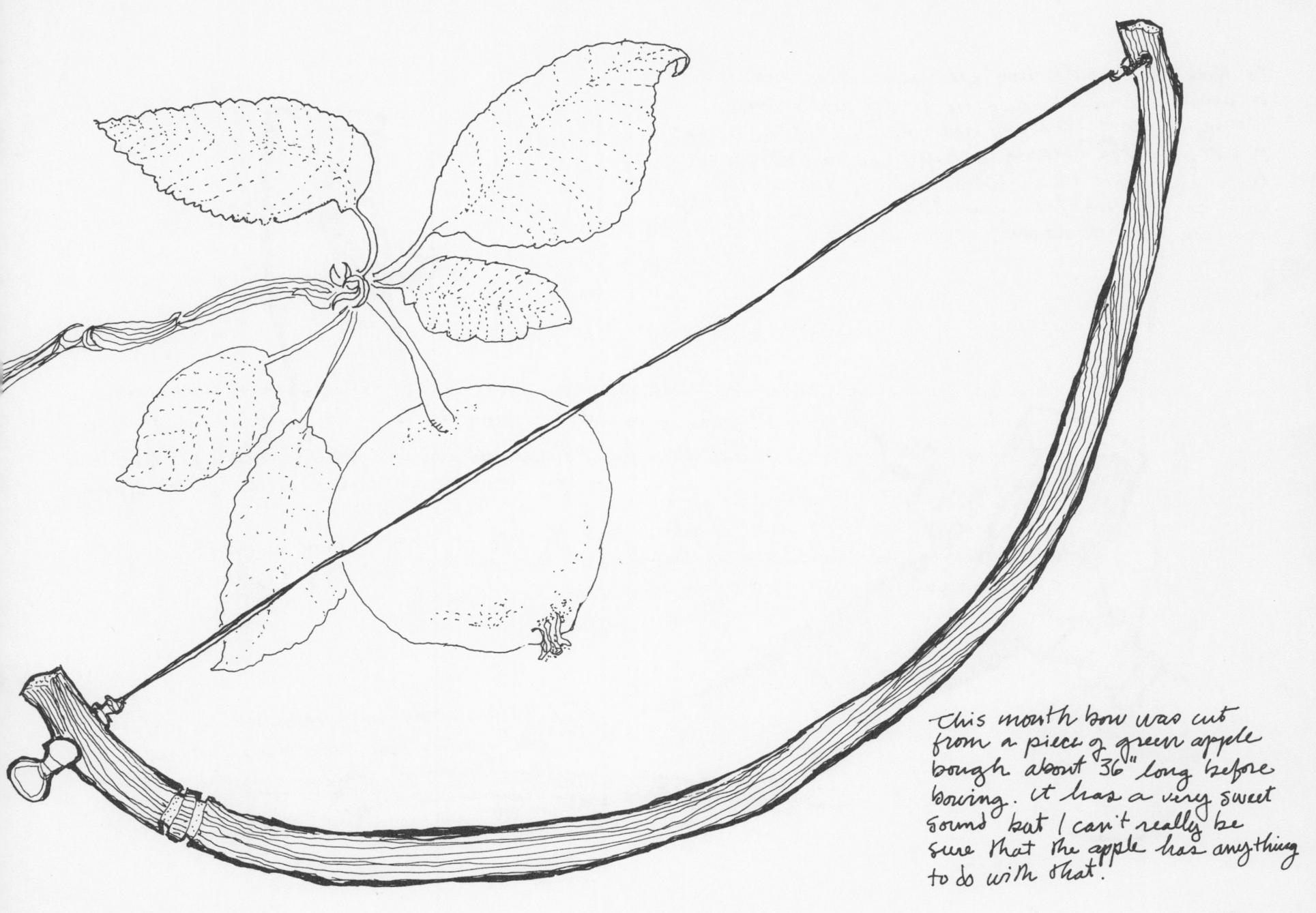

this mouth bow was cut
from a piece of green apple
bough about 36" long before
bowing. it has a very sweet
sound but I can't really be
sure that the apple has anything
to do with that.

9

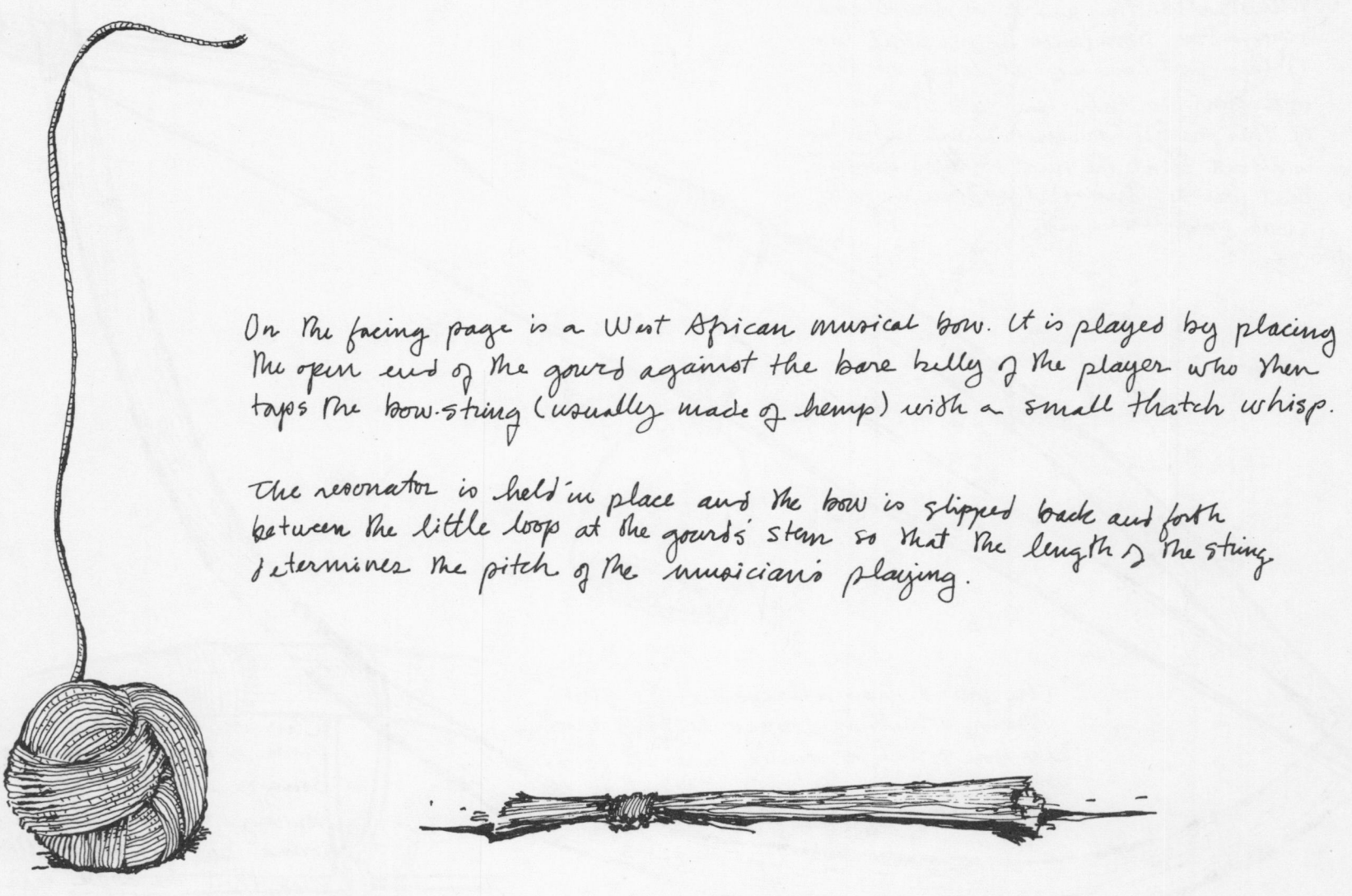

On the facing page is a West African musical bow. It is played by placing the open end of the gourd against the bare belly of the player who then taps the bow-string (usually made of hemp) with a small thatch whisp.

The resonator is held in place and the bow is slipped back and forth between the little loop at the gourd's stem so that the length of the string determines the pitch of the musician's playing.

This musical bow from the Congo
illustrates the use of a gourd as a
resonator. Sometimes a musical bow
of this sort can be as long as the
musician is tall but in the case
of this particular instrument - which
is about 4' at the most - I don't think
that was so. Unless it was an awfully
short musician.

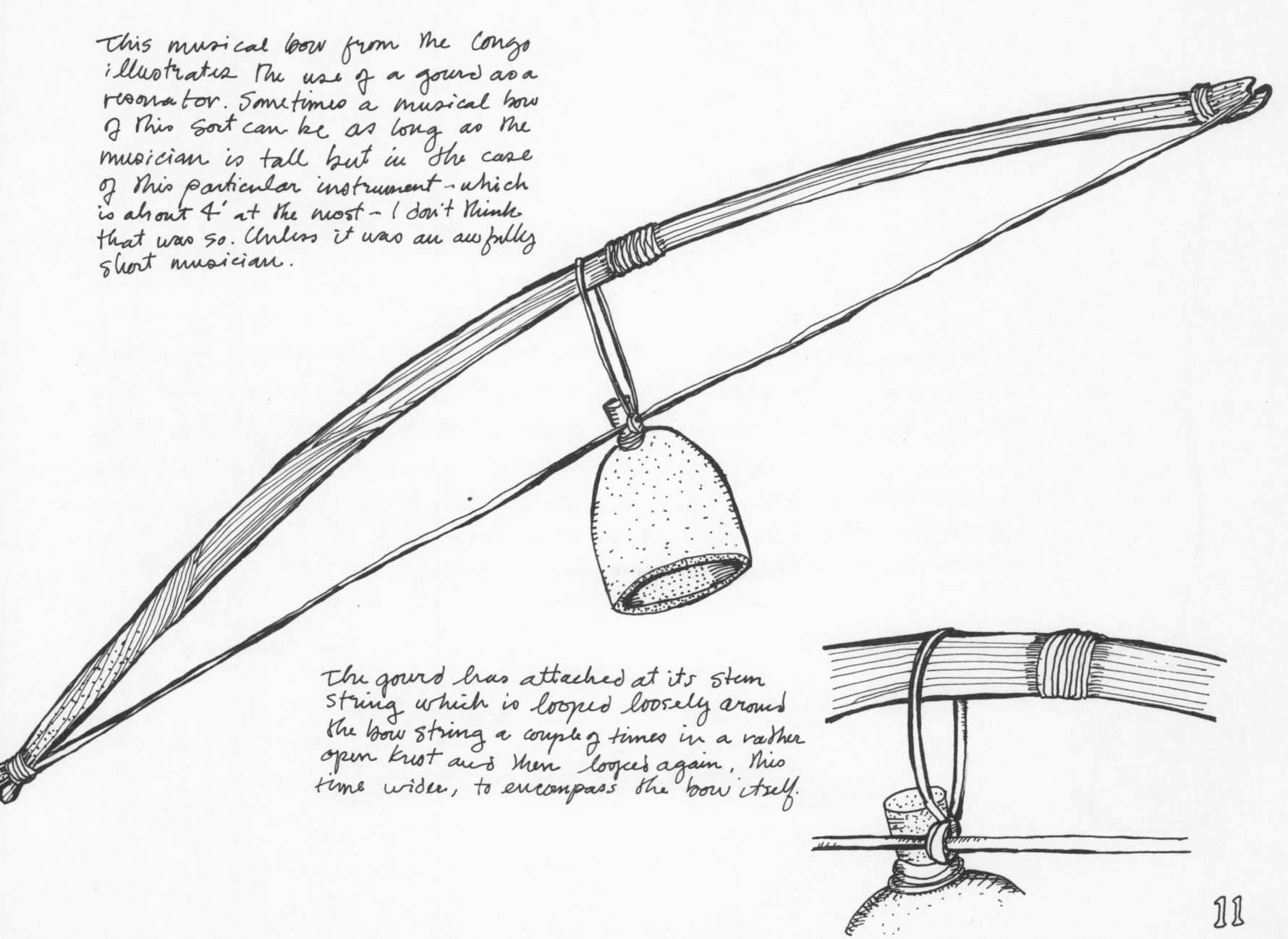

The gourd has attached at its stem
string which is looped loosely around
the bow string a couple of times in a rather
open knot and then looped again, this
time wider, to encompass the bow itself.

11

The Pluriare shown on the opposite page was made in Buzi, Liberia, of bamboo and a gourd sounding box. The tin rattle, which is typical of many African instruments, adds color tone to the musicians' playing. This instrument demonstrates the logical transition from the musical bow to the lyre.

The instrument is from the American Museum of Natural History, New York.

The poem is from Classical Black African Poems, selected and edited by Willard R. Trask and published by the Eakins Press, New York.

12

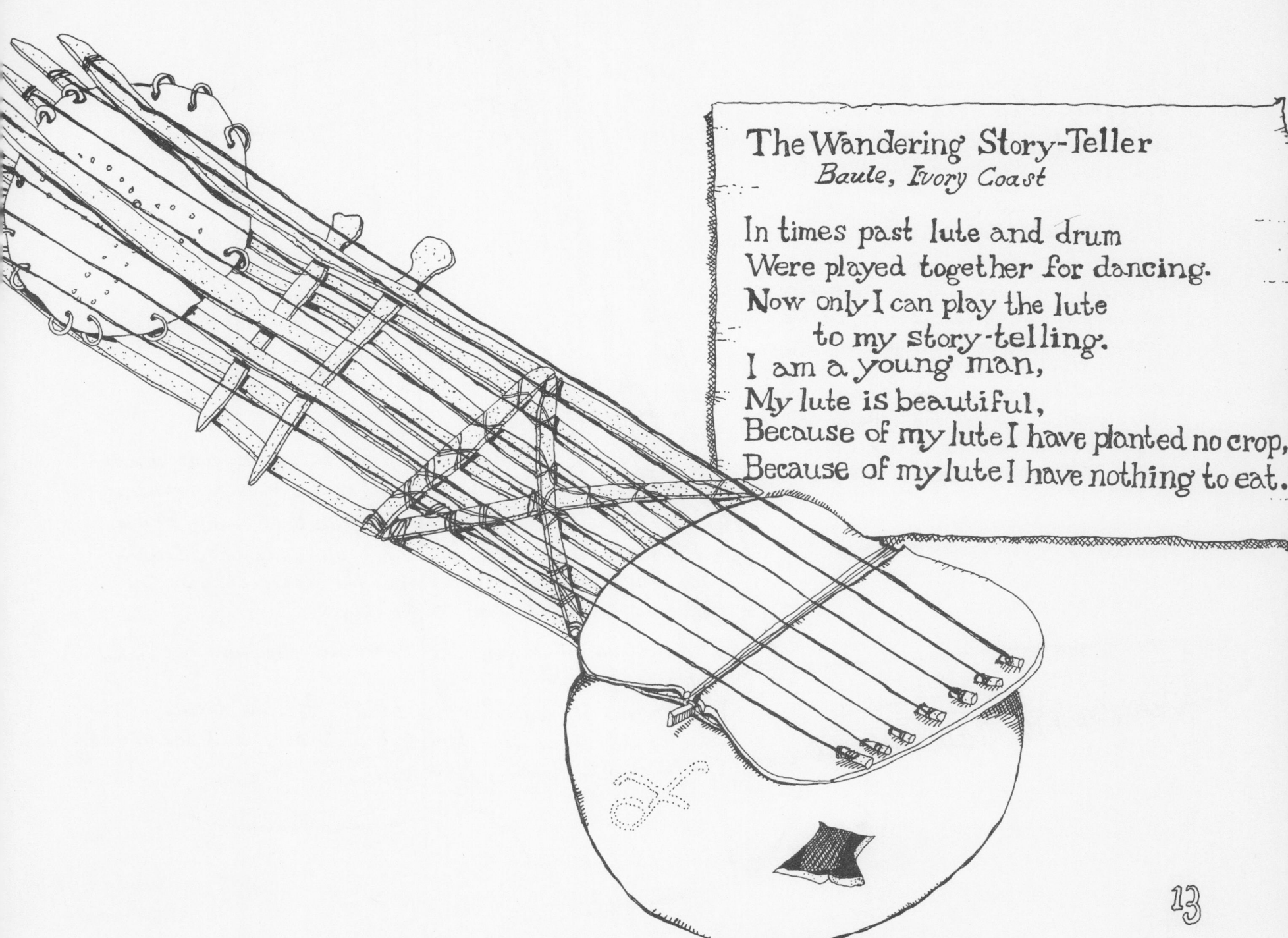

The Wandering Story-Teller
Baule, Ivory Coast

In times past lute and drum
Were played together for dancing.
Now only I can play the lute
    to my story-telling.
I am a young man,
My lute is beautiful,
Because of my lute I have planted no crop,
Because of my lute I have nothing to eat.

13

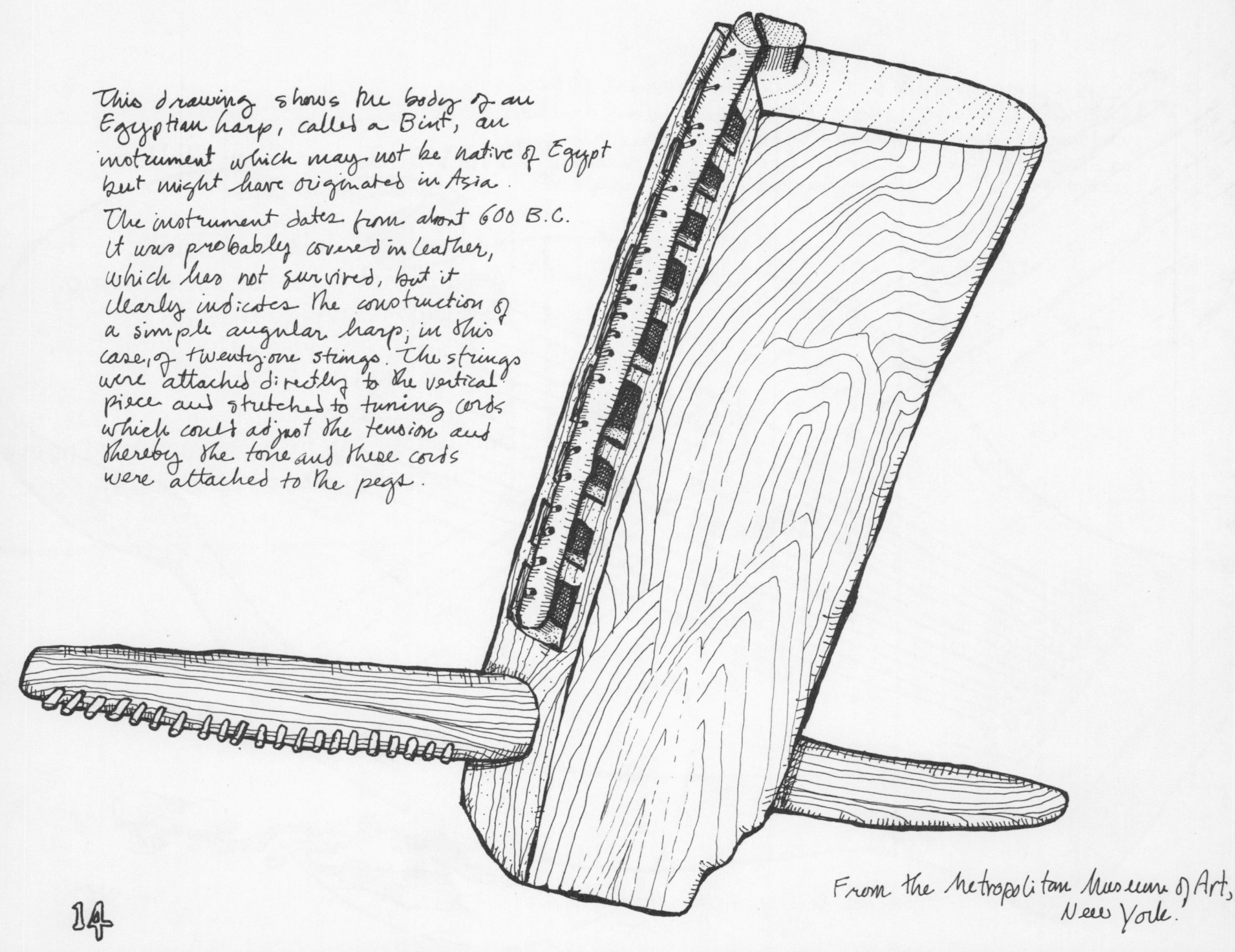

This drawing shows the body of an Egyptian harp, called a Bint, an instrument which may not be native of Egypt but might have originated in Asia.

The instrument dates from about 600 B.C. It was probably covered in leather, which has not survived, but it clearly indicates the construction of a simple angular harp; in this case, of twenty-one strings. The strings were attached directly to the vertical piece and stretched to tuning cords which could adjust the tension and thereby the tone and these cords were attached to the pegs.

From the Metropolitan Museum of Art, New York.

14

This is a very simple but handsome Japanese zither.
It would be easy to adapt this design to a homemade
instrument using commercially-manufactured zither pegs.
The wood is teak and would withstand the pressure
created by a tight-strung instrument such as a zither.

From the Metropolitan Museum of Art.
New York.

15

Another Zither, this one from Madagascar, is much more simple than the one on the previous page but I find it interesting for the use of cocanut as a resonator.

From the Metropolitan Museum of Art, New York.

16

Today, a Rebab, or Kamandja `adjúz, is played
to accompany folk singers in Egypt and West Africa.
This particular instrument also employs a cocanut
for a resonator, this one covered with hide.
The spike, which runs through the resonator,
enables the cocanut to be turned to facilitate bowing.

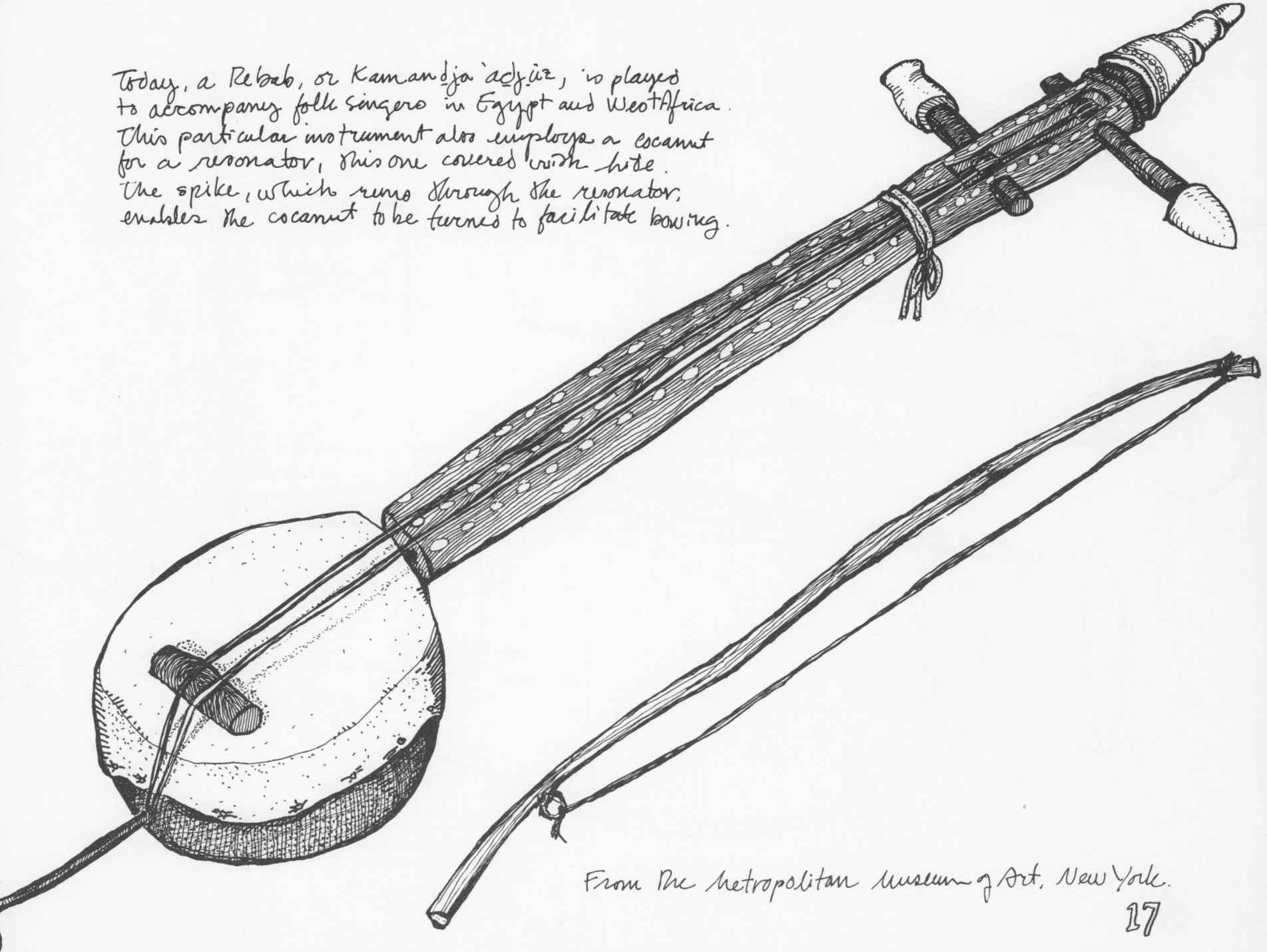

From the Metropolitan Museum of Art, New York.

17

The corn-stalk fiddle is an American folk toy instrument which does play a tune. Granted, you'll never make a concert stage with it but its just for fun. To make the fiddle (which is really more like a zither) you will need a section of green corn-stalk — the section between and including both joints. With a pen knife make an opening almost from the inside end of one joint to the other. This will give you built-in pegs for what will be your string. Cut only through the outer layer until you reach the fiber. Carefully pull a little bunch of this out and bridge it up with a twig or a little piece of wood. You can even make a bow if you like.

Just a caution: don't get too attached to your corn-stalk fiddle. It is a transitory joy and as it dries out will easily break.

The Agong is a tube zither from the Philippine Islands that closely resembles the corn stalk fiddle, or vice versa. It is made of a large section of bamboo and its two "strings" are both plucked and struck with a "hammer" made of a thin piece of bamboo. Needless to say, it is much less perishable than the instrument on the opposite page and certainly qualifies as a serious musical instrument.

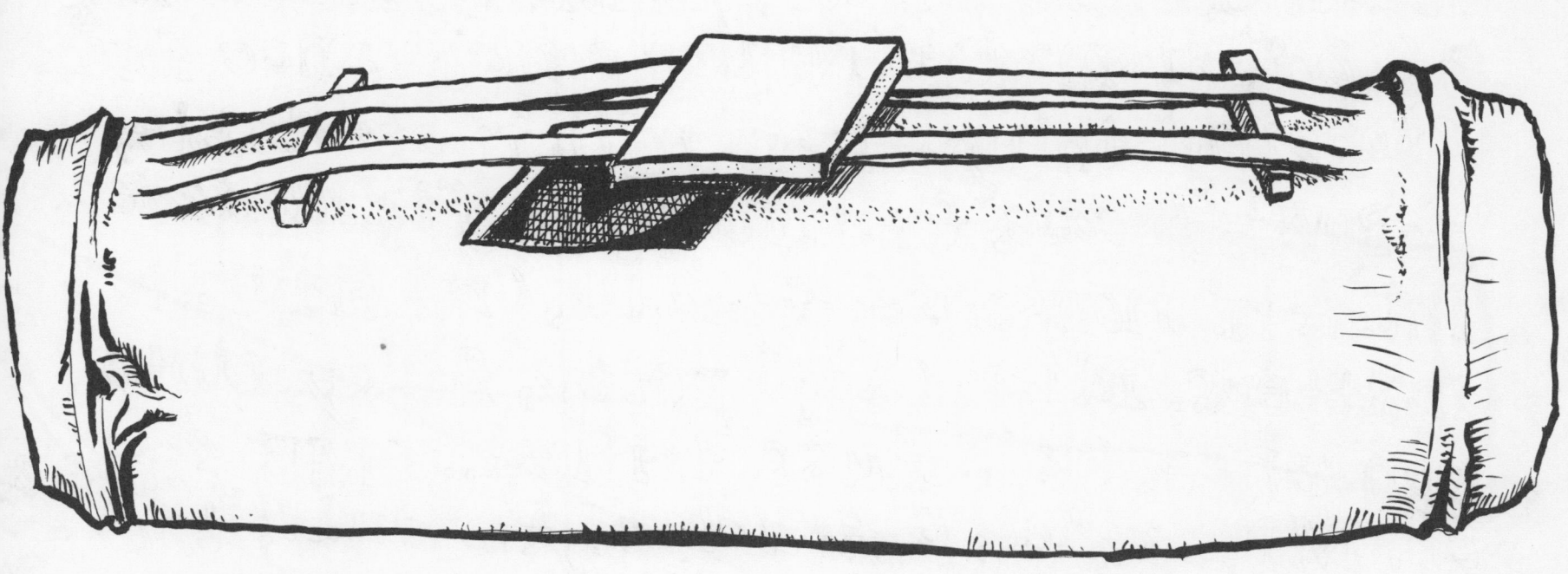

From the Metropolitan Museum of Art, New York.

fi·ddle, n., int., & v.i. & t. (Fam. or contempt. for) violin (*fit as a f.*, in good condition & spirits; *hang up one's f. when one comes home*, be witty abroad & dull at home; *play first, second, f.*, take leading, subordinate, position; *face as long as a f.*, dismal); (Naut.) contrivance for stopping things from rolling off table; *f.-bow*[1]; *f.-case*, for holding f.; fiddlededee, int. & n., nonsense; *f.-faddle*, (n.) trivial matters, idler, (adj.) petty, fussy, (int.) nonsense, (v.i.) fuss, trifle ... [ME *fithele*, cf. MDu. *vedel*, G *fiedel*, etym. dub.; there is med. L *vitula*, whence VIOL]

20

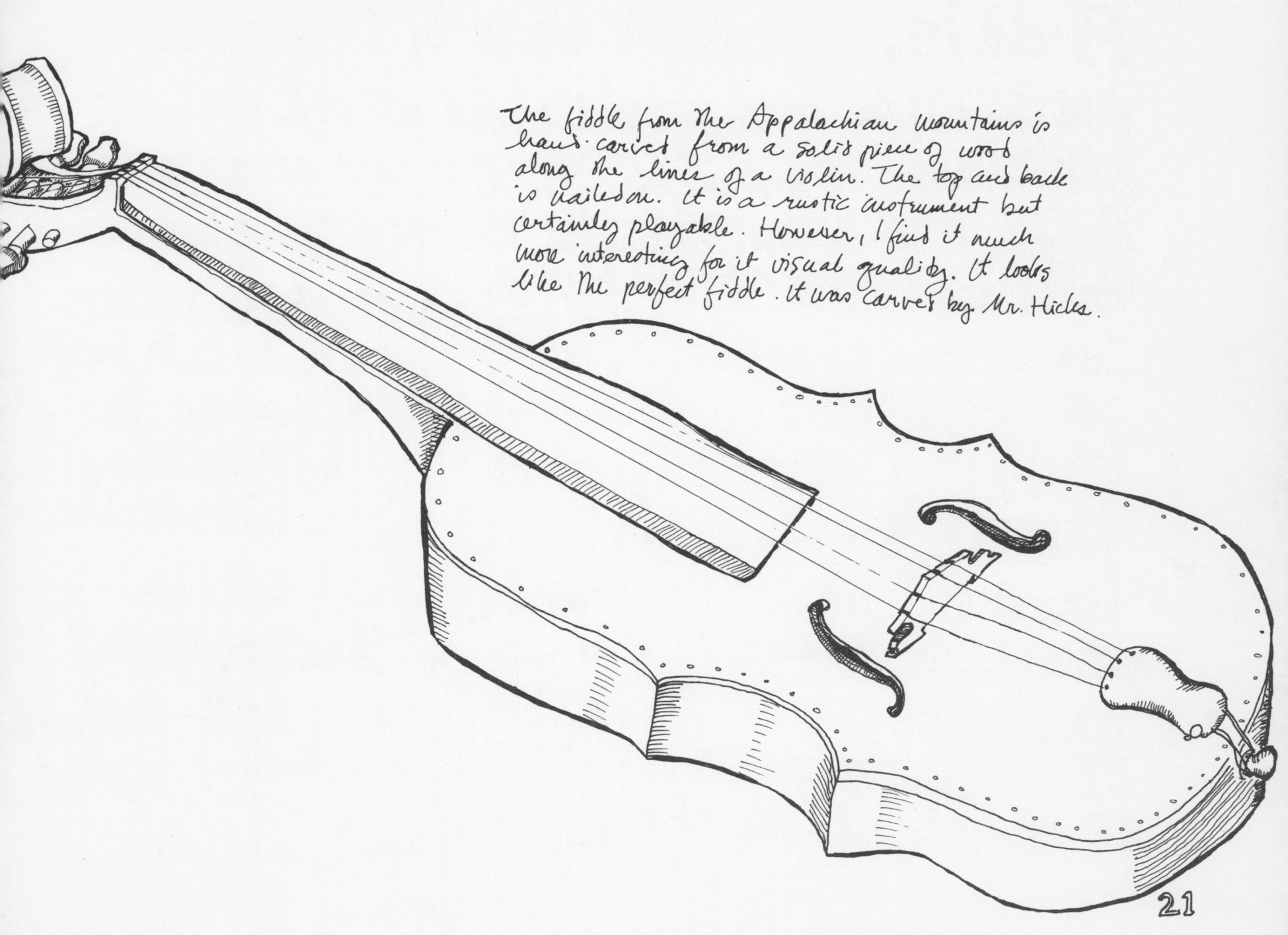

The fiddle from the Appalachian mountains is hand-carved from a solid piece of wood along the lines of a violin. The top and back is nailed on. It is a rustic instrument but certainly playable. However, I find it much more interesting for it visual quality. It looks like the perfect fiddle. It was carved by Mr. Hicks.

21

An instrument from Islamic North Africa is the Rebab.
It is played with a bow. This instrument, like the
Appalachian fiddle on the page before, was carved
from one piece of wood with the top and back applied.
The rebab is a probably ancestor of the fiddle and
probably the more musical sophisticated of instruments
from its area.

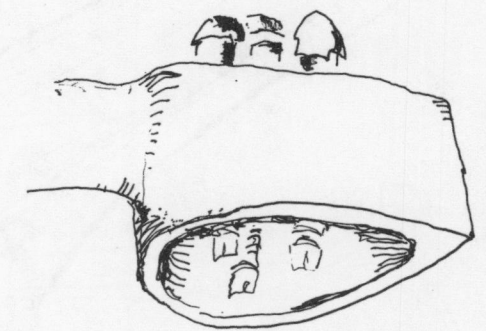

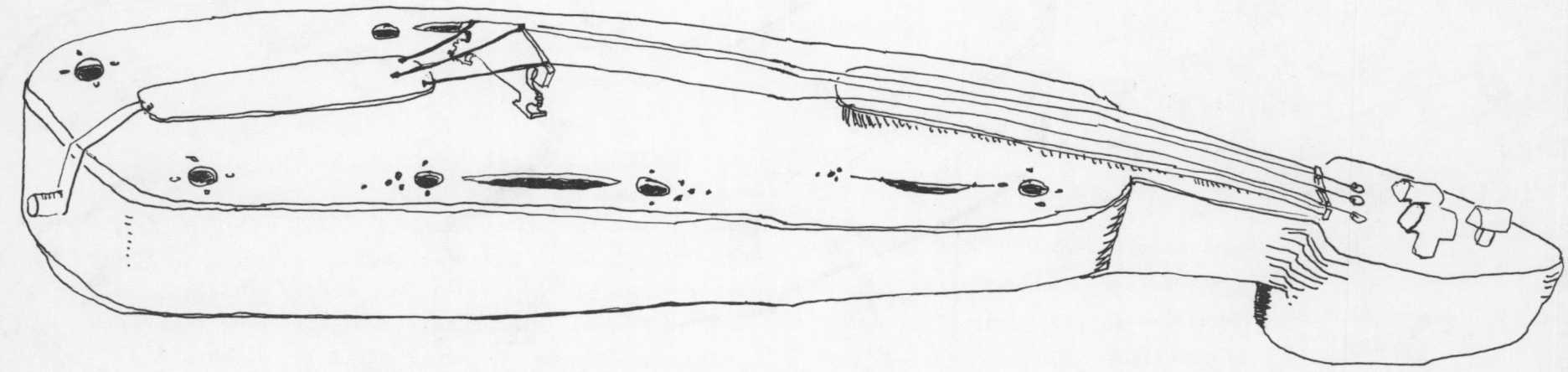

From the Metropolitan Museum of Art, New York.

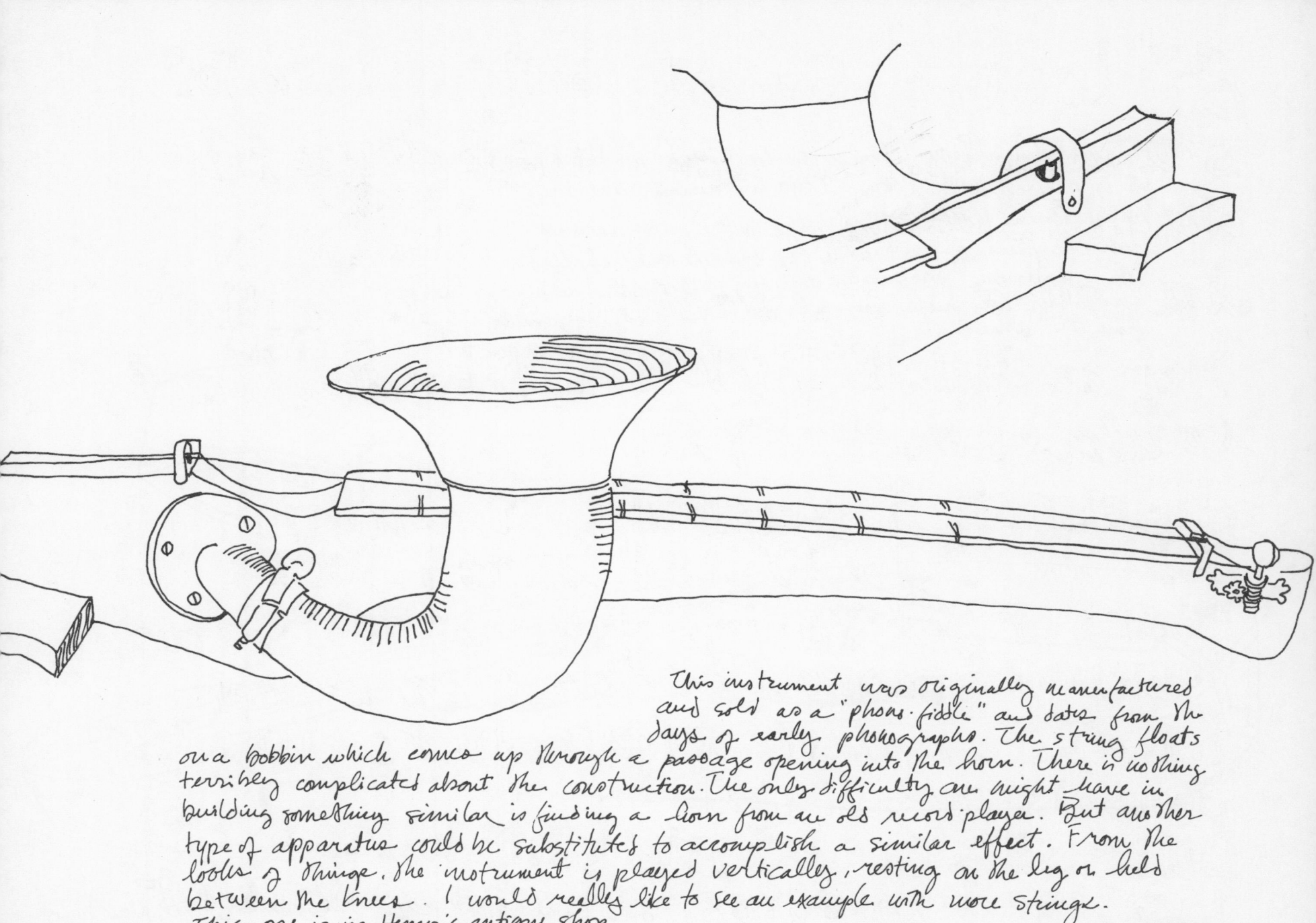

This instrument was originally manufactured and sold as a "phono-fiddle" and dates from the days of early phonographs. The string floats on a bobbin which comes up through a passage opening into the horn. There is nothing terribly complicated about the construction. The only difficulty one might have in building something similar is finding a horn from an old record player. But another type of apparatus could be substituted to accomplish a similar effect. From the looks of things, the instrument is played vertically, resting on the leg or held between the knees. I would really like to see an example with more strings. This one is in Henry's antique shop.

23

dŭl·cet, a. Sweet, soothing (esp. of sounds). [f. F doucet dim. of doux f. L dulcis sweet]

du·lcifȳ, v.t. Sweeten, make gentle. Hence dulciFICA·TION n. [f. L dulcificare (dulcis sweet, -FY)]

dŭlcimer, n. Musical instrument with strings of graduated length over sounding board or box struck with hammers, prototype of piano. [f. OF doulcimer perh. f. L dulce melos (not found in required sense) sweet tune]

Dŭlcinē·a (or -sĭ·nĭa), n. Idolized & idealized mistress. [name of Don Qui-

24

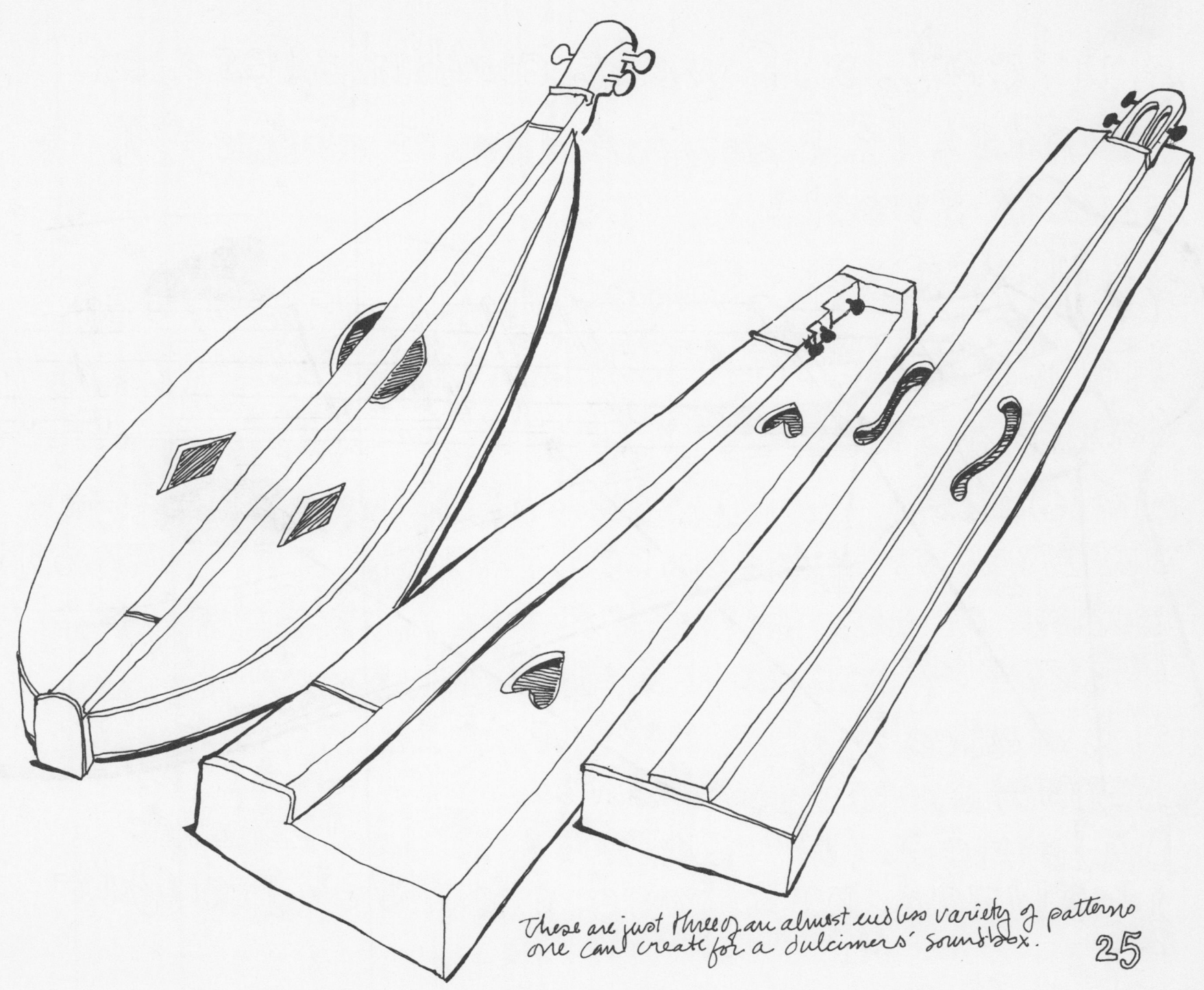

These are just three of an almost endless variety of patterns one can create for a dulcimers' soundbox.

25

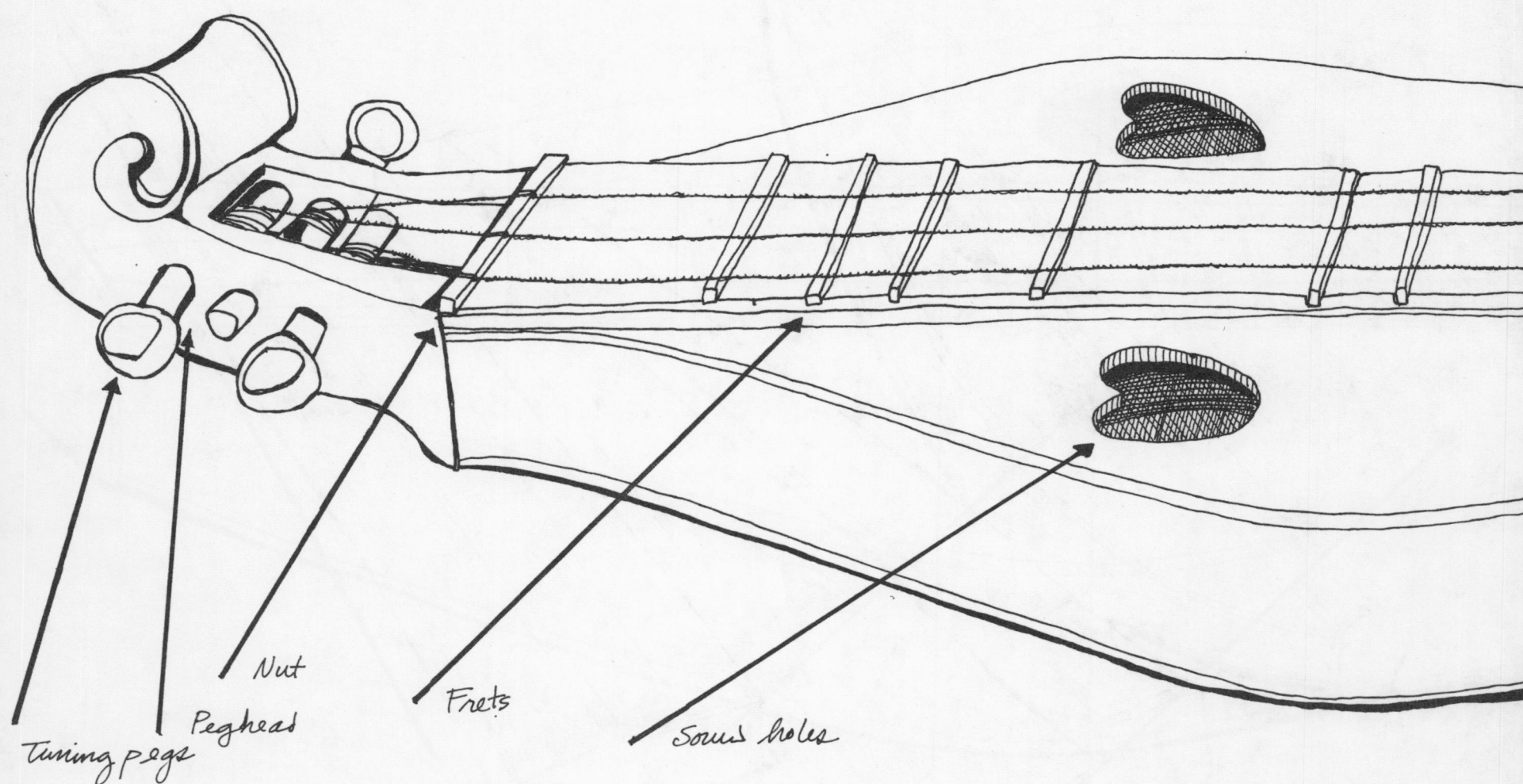

Nut

Peghead

Frets

Sound holes

Tuning pegs

26

The Parts of a Dulcimer

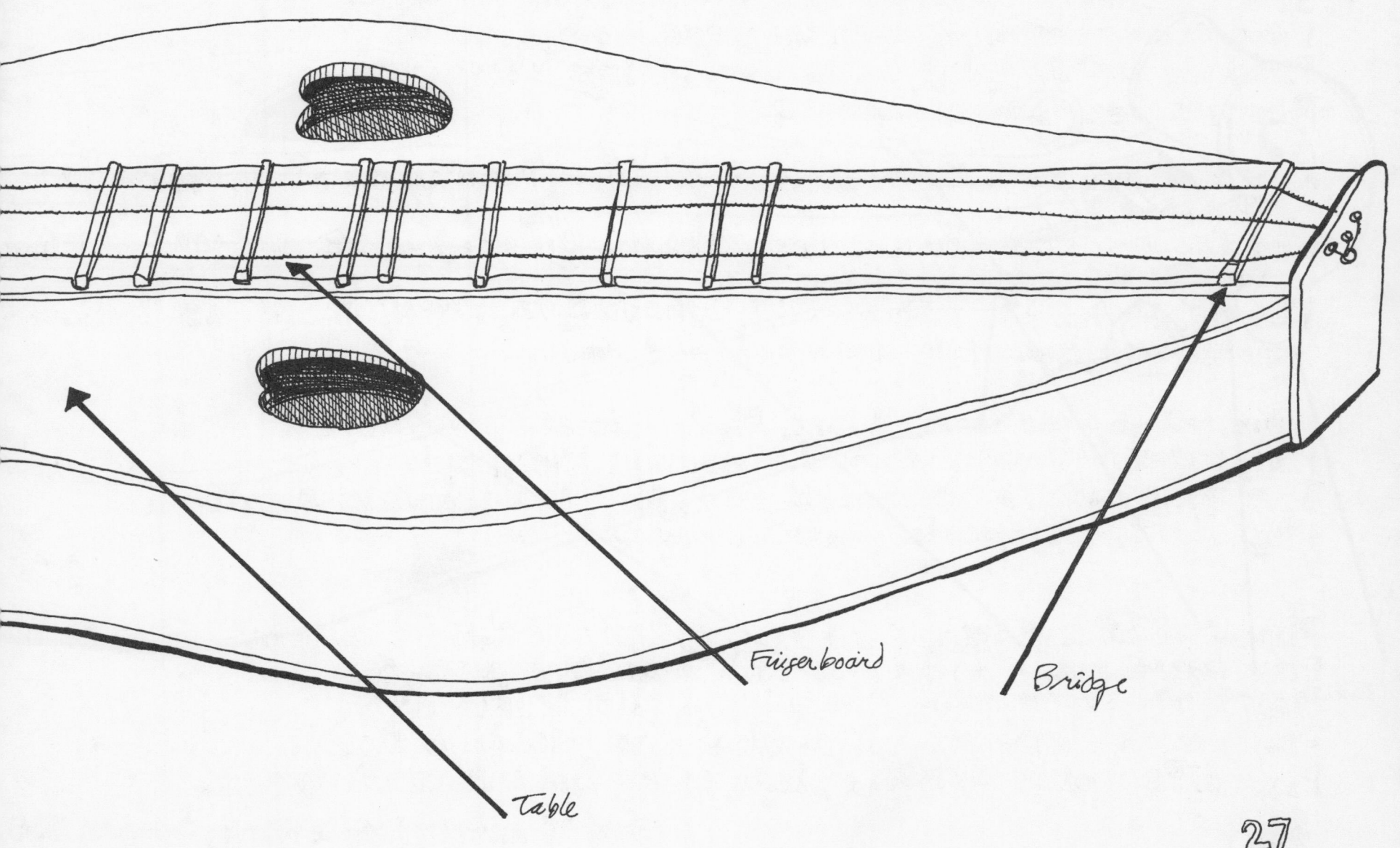

Fingerboard

Bridge

Table

Dulcimer
by James Still

The dulcimer's three strings are the heart's cords.
Tune them carefully, turn the pegs slowly,
Plucking and listening to the sweetening voice
Ringing clear and articulate.

Tune the first with the night, with shadows upon the mountain, approaching
    thunder,
The second with the morning, sheaves drowned in dew, sudden breaking
    of day,
The third with the midday sun, ripe-hanging, swollen and lush mellow.
Tune the strings carefully, turn the pegs slowly.

Strum and play the merry heart, high hope and laughter,
Play the child's thin voice, the wren in the maple tree,
The rain upon a clapboard roof, the undisolving shadow,
Play light, play dark, play unbound glee.

Play swiftening wings in narrow, predestined flight,
Play heartbreak on the outward wandering way,
Play time's slow evening, the quiet smile in sleep,
Play love's first waking, play the yielding light,
Play life, play death, play eyes that cannot weep.

From Mountain Life & Work; October, 1935.

There are, among dulcimers, two basic types. One, the hammered dulcimer, has a long and illustrious history in Europe. It seems to have come from Persia and wandered around through North Africa and Spain. Perhaps because of its portability it is an instrument found among often-moving peoples. It is, in a sense, a piano that can be carried on the back. For a long time, the hammered dulcimer has played an important part in Jewish folk-culture and it is an instrument that is frequently identified with Hungarian gypsies. This dulcimer has eighteen quadruple strings set on a shallow sound-box which is, more often than not, trapezoidal in shape. The instrument is played by striking the strings with a small hammer, hence its name and also the inspiration for the developement of what we know as the piano.

The other dulcimer, the one this book is more concerned with, is the Appalachian dulcimer. It is an instrument generally considered indigenous to North America and rather specifically to the Southern Appalachian Mountains, hence its name. This instrument has three strings (though some people build them with more, sometimes as many as eight); it is of simple construction and easy to play. The tone is delicate, suitable to accompaniment for the voice or with other types of instruments or with other dulcimers and it is naturally suited to the folk music that is often associated with the instrument.

Dulcimers are almost always considered "home made" though there are at least a few good craftsmen making them in or near almost every major city and I haven't met one yet who wasn't generous with tips and advice about dulcimer-making. It is an instrument that just sort of naturally makes friends.

29

The patterns of a dulcimer's soundbox vary with the maker's artistry and ingenuity though the fiddle-type pictured on the pages illustrating the instruments' parts is probably the more characteristic Appalachian dulcimer with the heart-shaped sound-holes. The part of the dulcimer that is necessary to detail is the finger-board which is the real backbone of the instrument. As a matter of fact, you don't even need a sound box if the fingerboard is right. A table will do nicely.

Woods that are traditionally used in dulcimer-making are walnut, cherry and maple, usually in combination. Other good woods are chestnut, butternut, sassafras, sumac, cedar, pine and poplar.

You can use the commercially manufactured, ready-made pegs and frets that are available in musical supply houses and some hobby shops but the "real" ones are whittled out. If the peg tends to slip, moisten it a little to get the wood to expand. Better yet, a little resin, worked into the peg-hole and around the peg will cure the slipping.

Make your own frets from broom maker's wire or heavy copper wire. Bend the wire with pliers to form a staple and cut the ends at a sharp angle. Hammer them down. Wire nails, filed down at the head, make good frets. A whittled-down pocket comb is a good source for the bridge and nut.

One tool I've run across which is handy in many types of musical instrument making is a homemade fiddle clamp made from old wooden spools. The plastic version has almost made wooden spools antiques but when you find them - try junk stores - this diagram shows you what you can do.

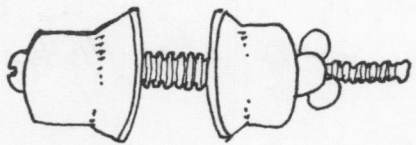 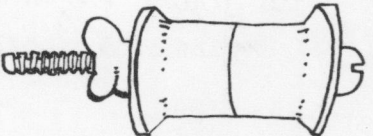

the fretting pattern for your dulcimer

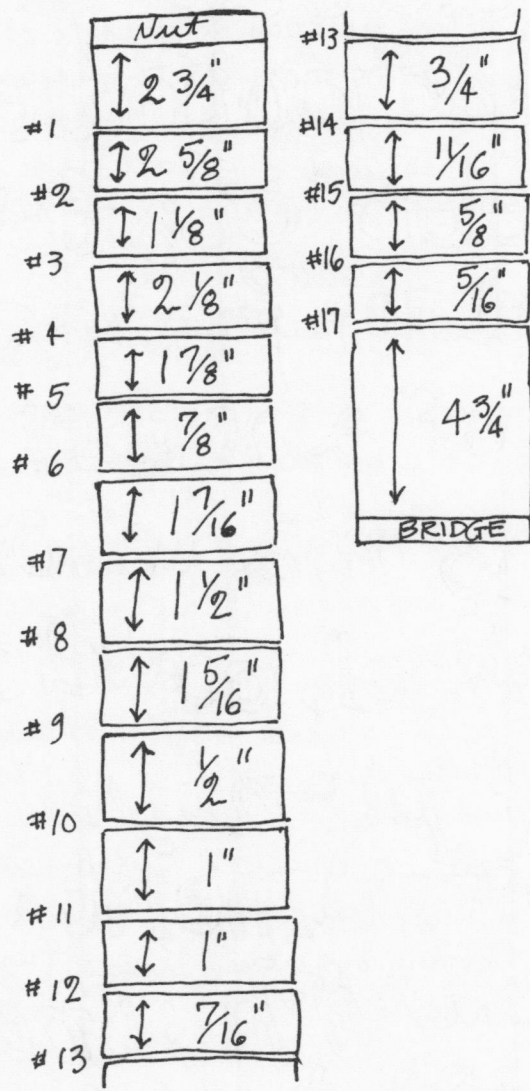

Nut

#1 — 2 3/4"
#2 — 2 5/8"
#3 — 1 7/8"
#4 — 2 1/8"
#5 — 1 7/8"
#6 — 7/8"
#7 — 1 7/16"
#8 — 1 1/2"
#9 — 1 5/16"
#10 — 1/2"
#11 — 1"
#12 — 1"
#13 — 7/16"

#13 — 3/4"
#14 — 1 1/16"
#15 — 5/8"
#16 — 5/16"
#17 — 4 3/4"

BRIDGE

Dulcimer-making is pretty much an improvisational sort of thing. You can invent just about any kind of sound box you like. But the one thing that is "fixed" is the finger-board's fretting pattern.

this is something you'll have to follow the directions on.

Cut a piece of brown paper exactly as long and as wide as the fingerboard. That should be 1 1/2" x 36". I am allowing longer than necessary for any fancy work you might do for the peg-head and for waste.

When you've marked down the pattern according to the measurements given secure the paper to the board and pick through with a pin, like this ...., across the width. This will give you a good mark to cut into when you are ready to lay down your frets.

horn[1], n. Non-deciduous excr- scence, often curved & pointed, on head of cattle, sheep, goats, & other mammals, found in pairs, single, or one in front of another; ta- the BULL[1] by the hh.; thing made of h. as SHOE-h.; drinking-vessel, powder- flask, made of h.; h. of plenty, = CORNUCOPIA; wind instrument (not now made of h.), as hunting-h., Frenc- h. (of trumpet class), English-h. (kind of oboe); extremity of moon or

The Shofar is one of the most ancient
musical instruments still used today
in Jewish worships.

The instructions on the next several
pages describe the making of a
shofar.

The instructions which follow, while describing
how to make a shofar, may also be used
for making any end or side-blown instrument
from horn.

Saw the horn at the point of the arrow.
The portion to the right is not useable.

33

The first step in making a horn
is to boil it. This will take some
time and careful watching from
time to time. Tie the horn at the
tip and suspend it into the boiling
water. Do not boil the entire horn,
as that might soften the outer
shell and cause problems later. What
you want to accomplish in this step
is to soften all of the material
inside the horn so that it may be
removed more easily.
The neighbours thought I was making
a very strange soup when I did this.
It is best to do it with the windows
open. Also try to avoid using your
best cooking pot.

34

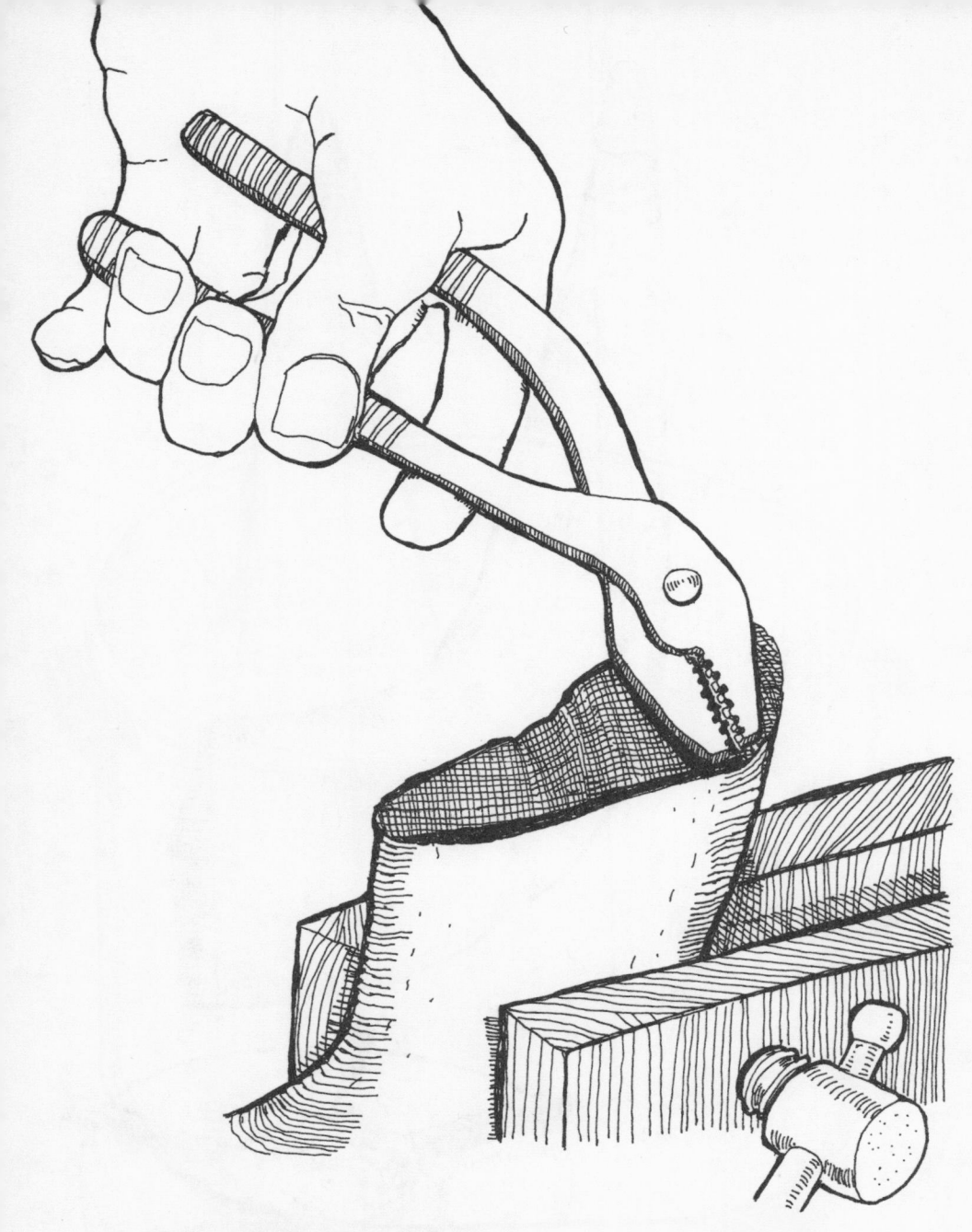

After chucking a few times, you'll find the bony material inside the horn soft enough to remove. You'll need a good vice or clamp for this and work while the horn is still hot. With pliers and a pick remove everything you can and then scrape out anything that might be left.

It may be necessary to return the horn to boiling water. The important thing is to make certain that the horn is free of all unwanted material and clean. Any roughness can be sanded or filed down later.

While it is important to have the horn clean it is also equally important to have the horn intact. Stop as soon as you've accomplished this step.

35

When I came to this step making my horn
I used a coat-hanger contraption — as I
did when I boiled the horn in the first
step. It saves cooking your arm.

The object here is to heat the horn enough
to make it pliable.

Do not burn the horn in the process.

Use a low flame. The horn will blister
if the flame is too high.

The horn will be very warm but not hot
when it is pliable enough for the next
step.

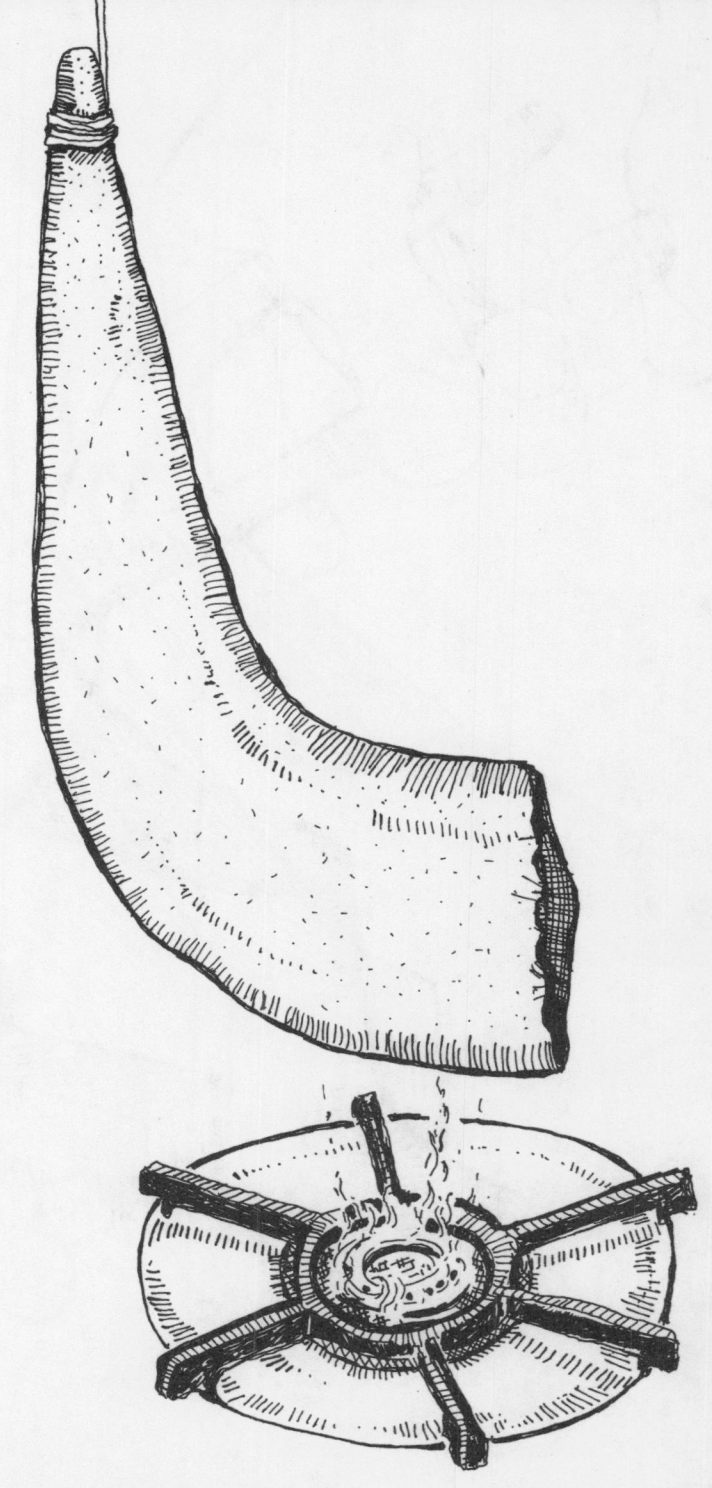

36

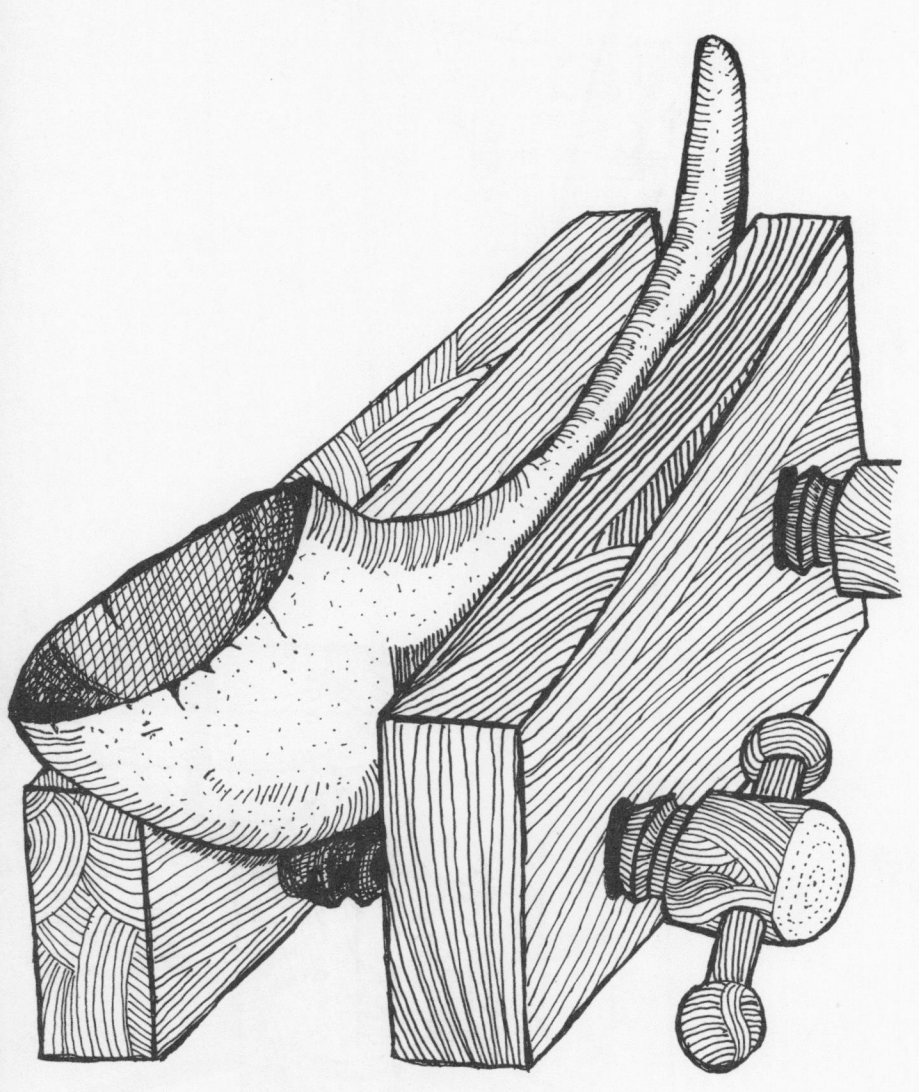

Return the warm horn to a clamp
or vice and apply pressure.
You are straightening out any
unusual curves and making the
shape more uniform.
After the horn has cooled and has
been pressed for a while, return it
to the heat and remove another
imperfect curve.
Repeat this process till you have
the desired shape of your
instrument.

Next, with a power drill, make an opening at the tip of the horn. This should be done carefully to meet as perfectly with the natural hollow as possible.
A 1/8" drill bit is large enough.

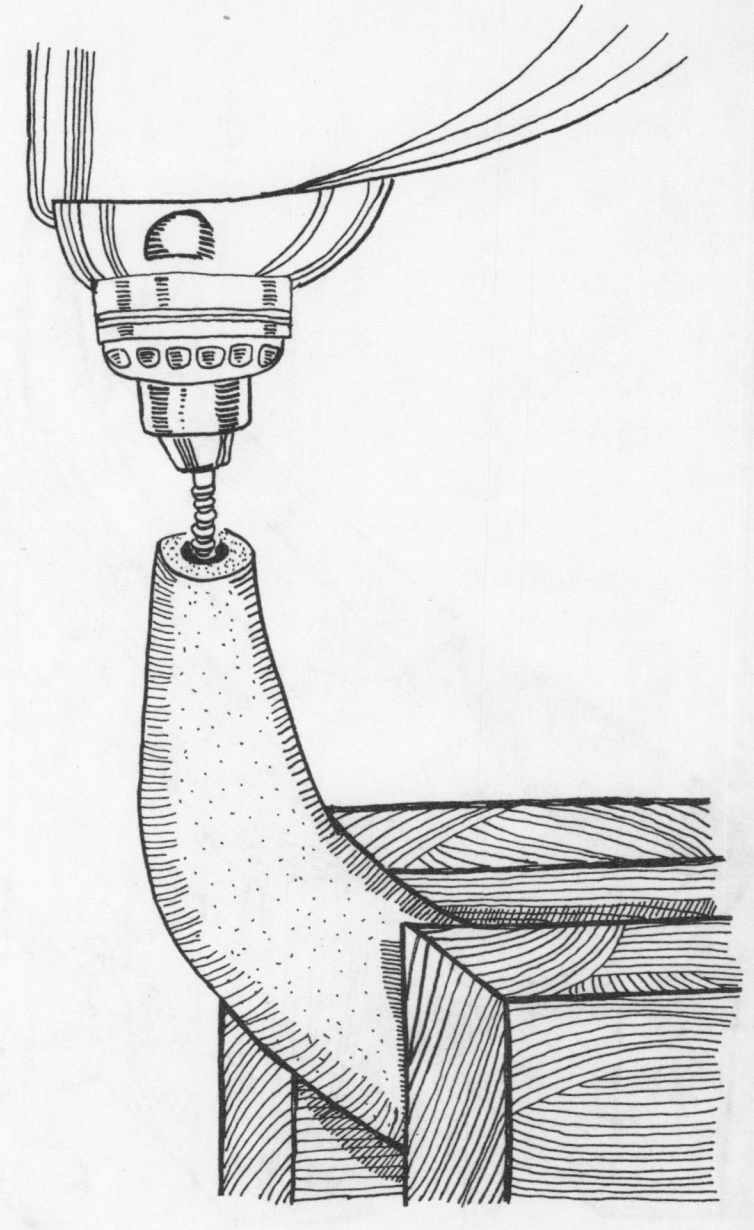

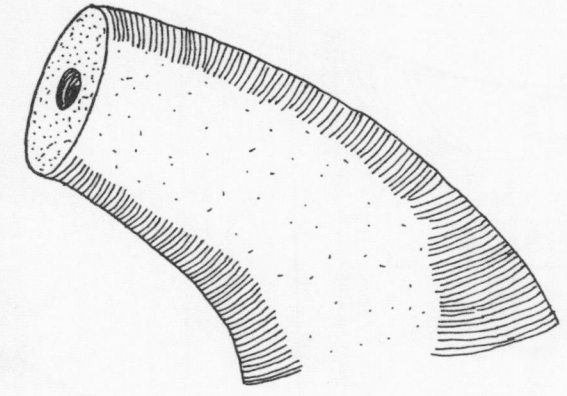

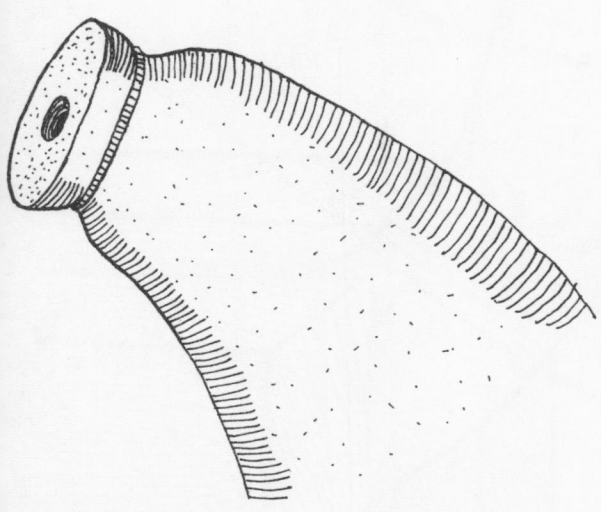

The next step requires a strong,
sharp knife and an eye for design.
Create a mouthpiece as you like.
The main qualification is that it
should not have sharp edges
and that it be easy to blow into.

At this point you have a horn —
or a shofar — ready to be sounded.

With care and attention, it should last
for many generations. It is
generally adviseable to moisten the
instrument from time to time to keep
it from cracking, and certainly a
day or two before playing.

A coronet may be carved at the end
or decoration applied or incised.

The shofar is one of the oldest Biblical musical instruments still in regular use and manufactured in much the same manner as it always has been.
This particular example is from Bohemia, from the Eighteenth or Nineteenth Century.
The inscription in Hebrew means:

"Blow the horn at the new moon,
at the new moon,
for our feast day."

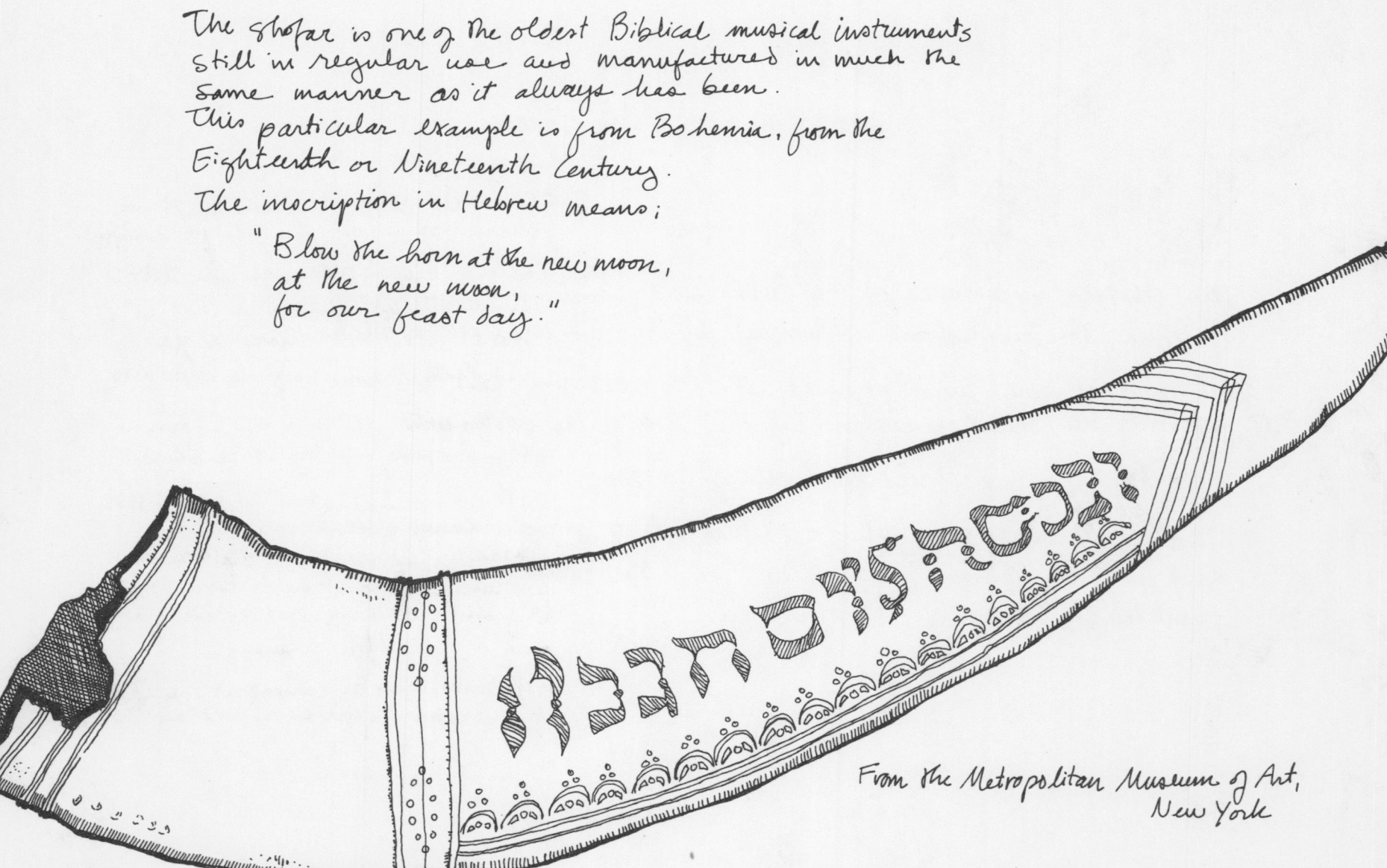

תקעו בחדש שופר בכסה ליום חגנו

From the Metropolitan Museum of Art,
New York

40

The shofars' appearance in the Bible is a single but mighty one. Joshua, the Judge, was commanded by the Lord to attack Jericho.

With him were seven priests, all with shofarim and they were followed in their procession by the Ark of the Covenant.

For six days they circled the walls of the city.

On the seventh day they circled the city of Jericho seven times and as they strode, they blew. "and the walls came tumbling down."

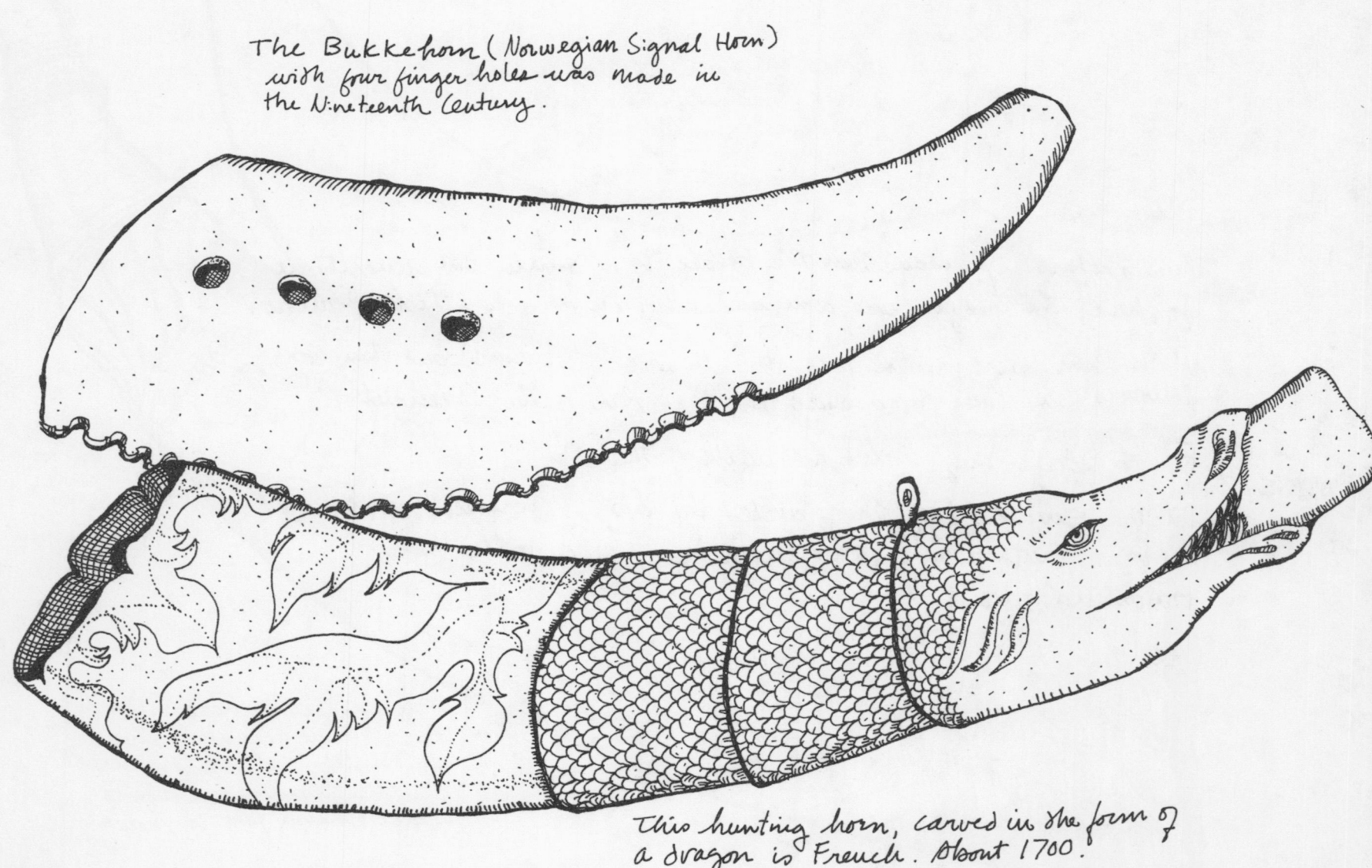

The Bukkehorn (Norwegian Signal Horn)
with four finger holes was made in
the Nineteenth Century.

This hunting horn, carved in the form of
a dragon is French. About 1700.

From the Metropolitan Museum of Art, New York.

There is evidence of ox horns, carved and decorated with gold, dating to 1400 B.C. in Egypt.

This ox horn, sitting on my desk, came from a cow pasture somewhere.

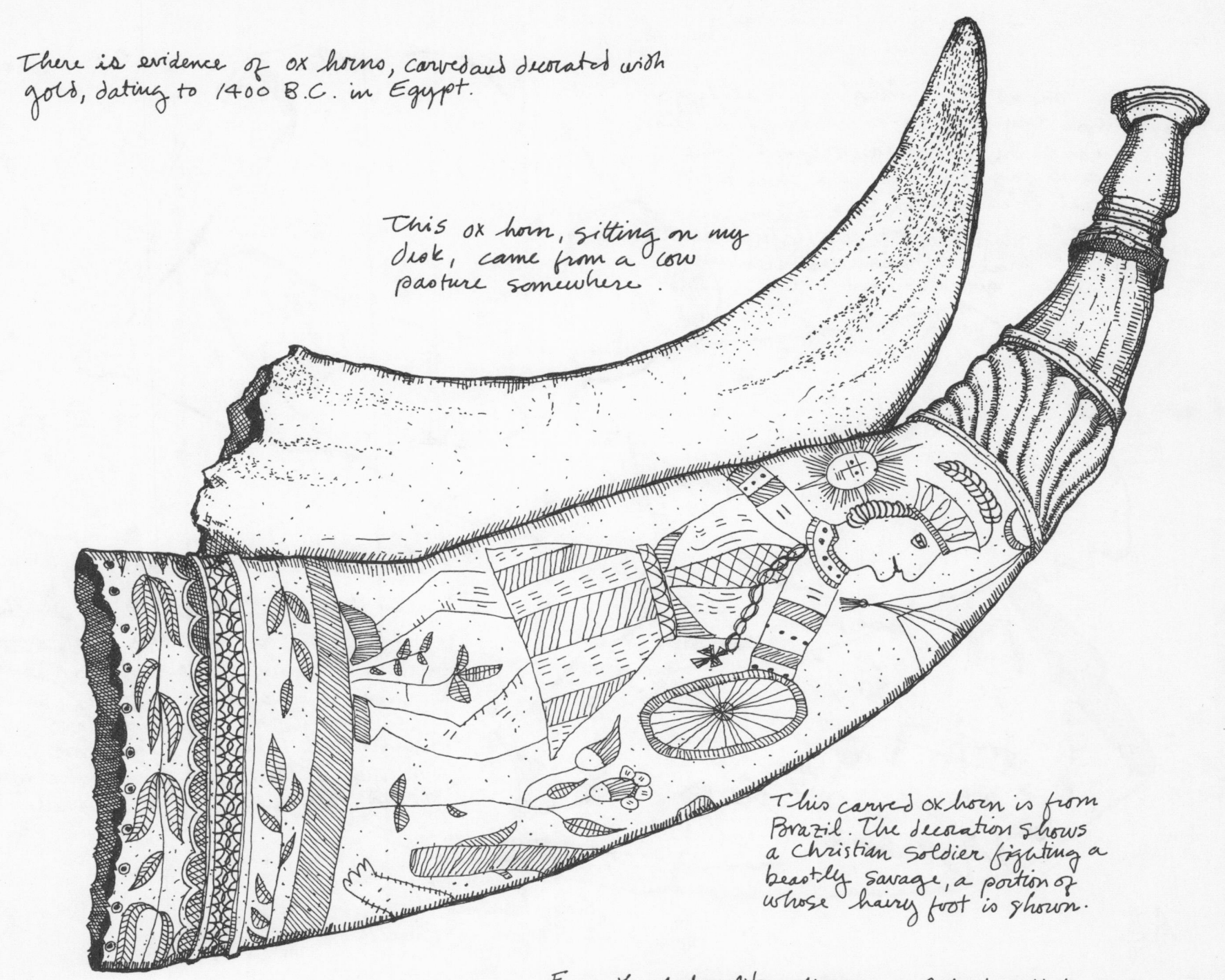

This carved ox horn is from Brazil. The decoration shows a Christian soldier fighting a beastly savage, a portion of whose hairy foot is shown.

From the Metropolitan Museum of Art, New York.

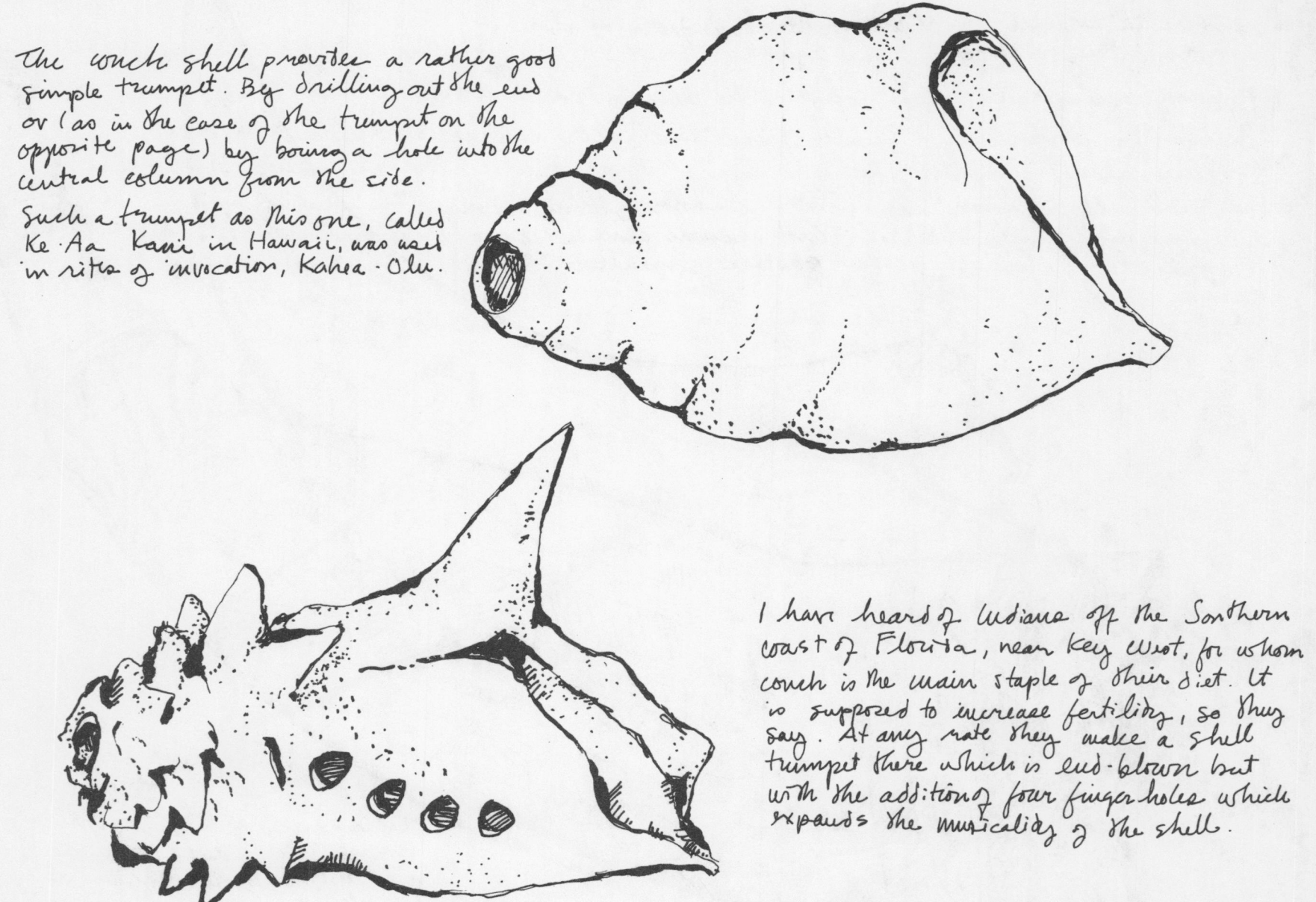

The conch shell provides a rather good
simple trumpet. By drilling out the end
or (as in the case of the trumpet on the
opposite page) by boring a hole into the
central column from the side.

Such a trumpet as this one, called
Ke·Aa·Kani in Hawaii, was used
in rites of invocation, Kahea·Olu.

I have heard of Indians off the Southern
coast of Florida, near Key West, for whom
conch is the main staple of their diet. It
is supposed to increase fertility, so they
say. At any rate they make a shell
trumpet there which is end-blown but
with the addition of four finger holes which
expands the musicality of the shell.

44

In many ancient and tribal societies the playing of a conch shell was strictly reserved for women only. Because it was from water and the water and the moon are so often given feminine characteristics, it has a special magical quality. It has been used in many moon-related rites, given authority over the weather and the seas and often the harvest. There are instances in some areas of Central Europe today where the conch shell trumpet is sounded to quell thunderstorms. Whether it does this or not is beyond my judgement. I can say that the sound of such a trumpet can almost rival a thunderstorm.

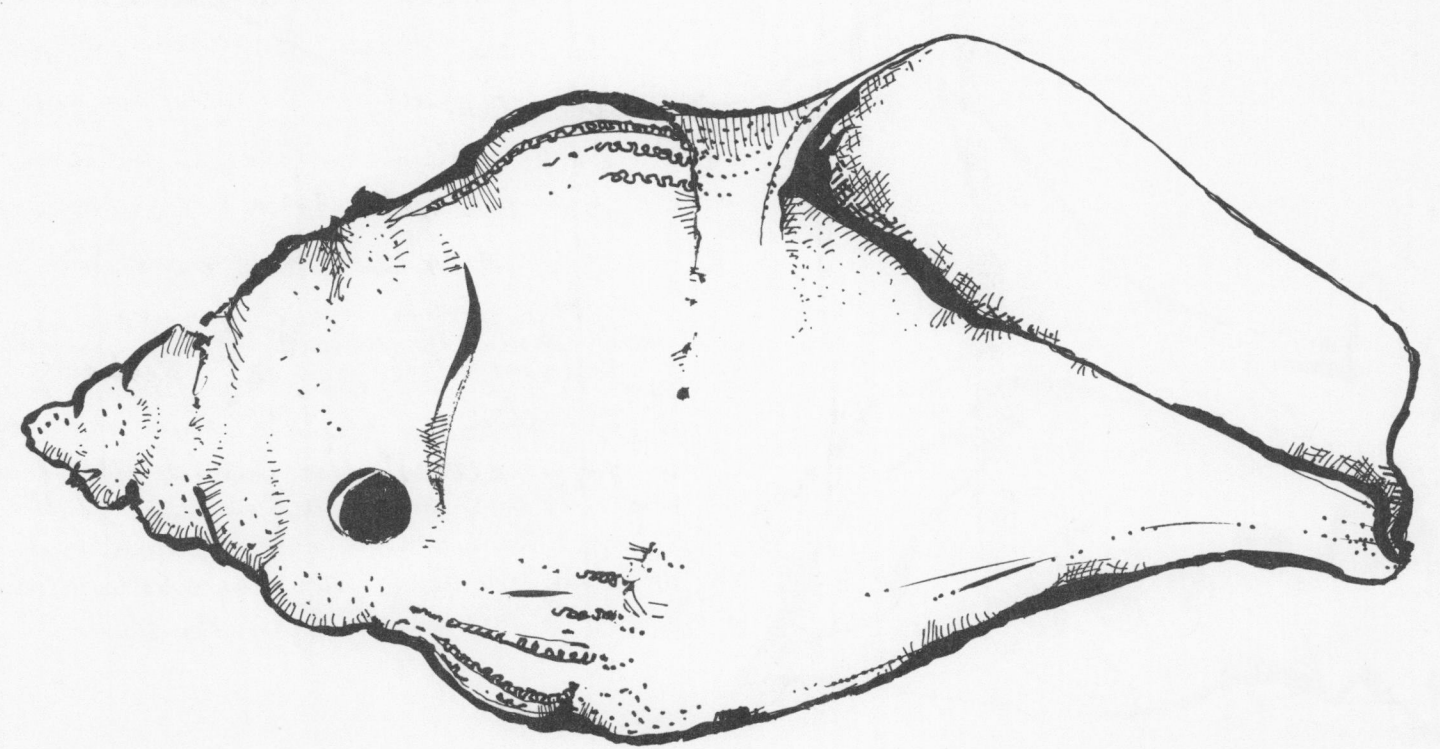

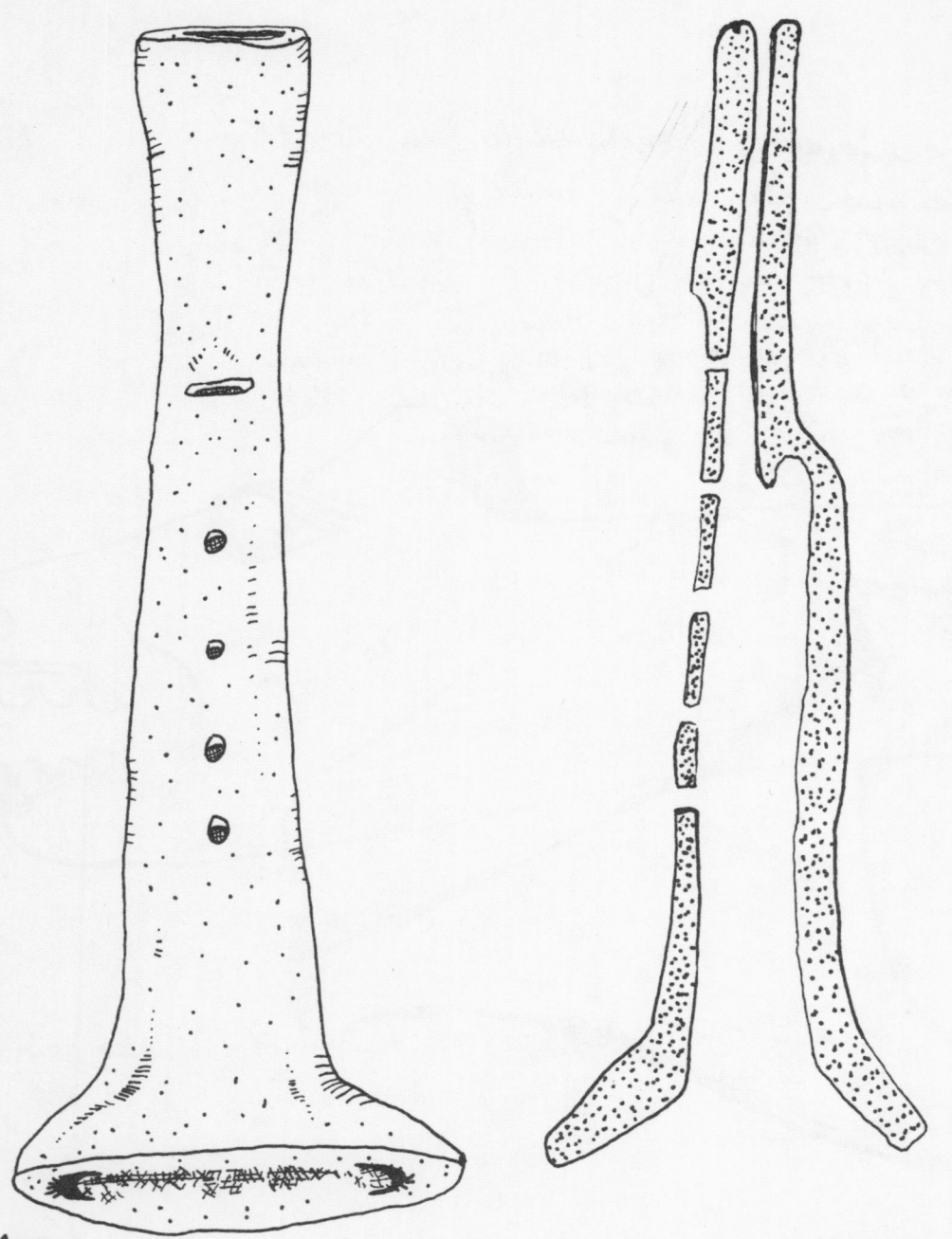

This flute-like whistle is made
of clay. The diagram suggests
its construction. The finger-holes
do not follow a special pattern
and the bell doesn't function.
It is Mexican and probably an
attempt to copy a Spanish
musical instrument, perhaps
an oboe.
It is, nevertheless, fun to make.

46

This clay trumpet is from Peru. It suggests
one of the two types of trumpets used in the
Americas before European colonization. The
other, an end-blow trumpet made of shell,
is like others of the same type shown on page

It would be easy to make this trumpet.
Perhaps not so easy would be playing it.

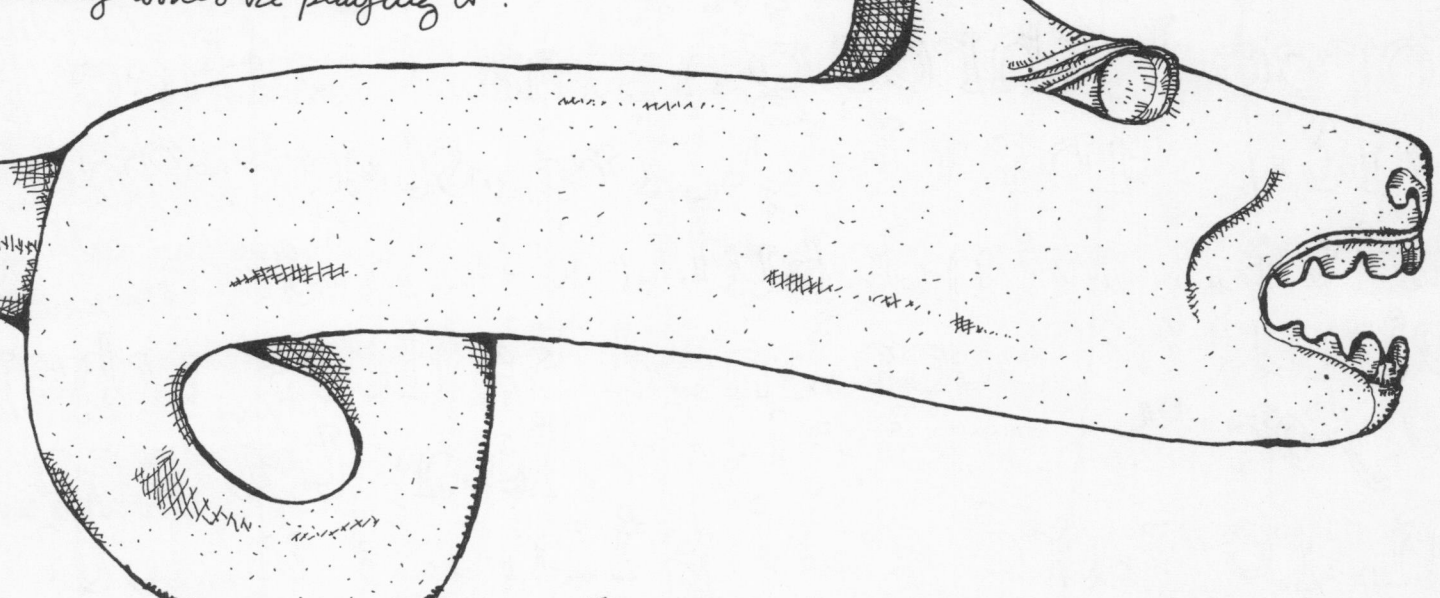

From the Metropolitan Museum of Art, New York.

47

whi·stle (-sl), v.i. & t., & n. Make with the lips or with instrument for the purpose, or (of birds &c.) with the voice, or (of missile, wind, &c.) by rapi motion, the shrill sound of breath forced through small orifice formed with lips (boy, bird, steam-engine or its driver, wind, bullet, whistles; w. for a wind, of becalmed sailors, whence may w. for it, vainly wish; let one go w., disregard his wishes; whistling, in names of kinds of bird and animal) (N.) whistling sound or note; instrume. for producing such sound (penny w.,

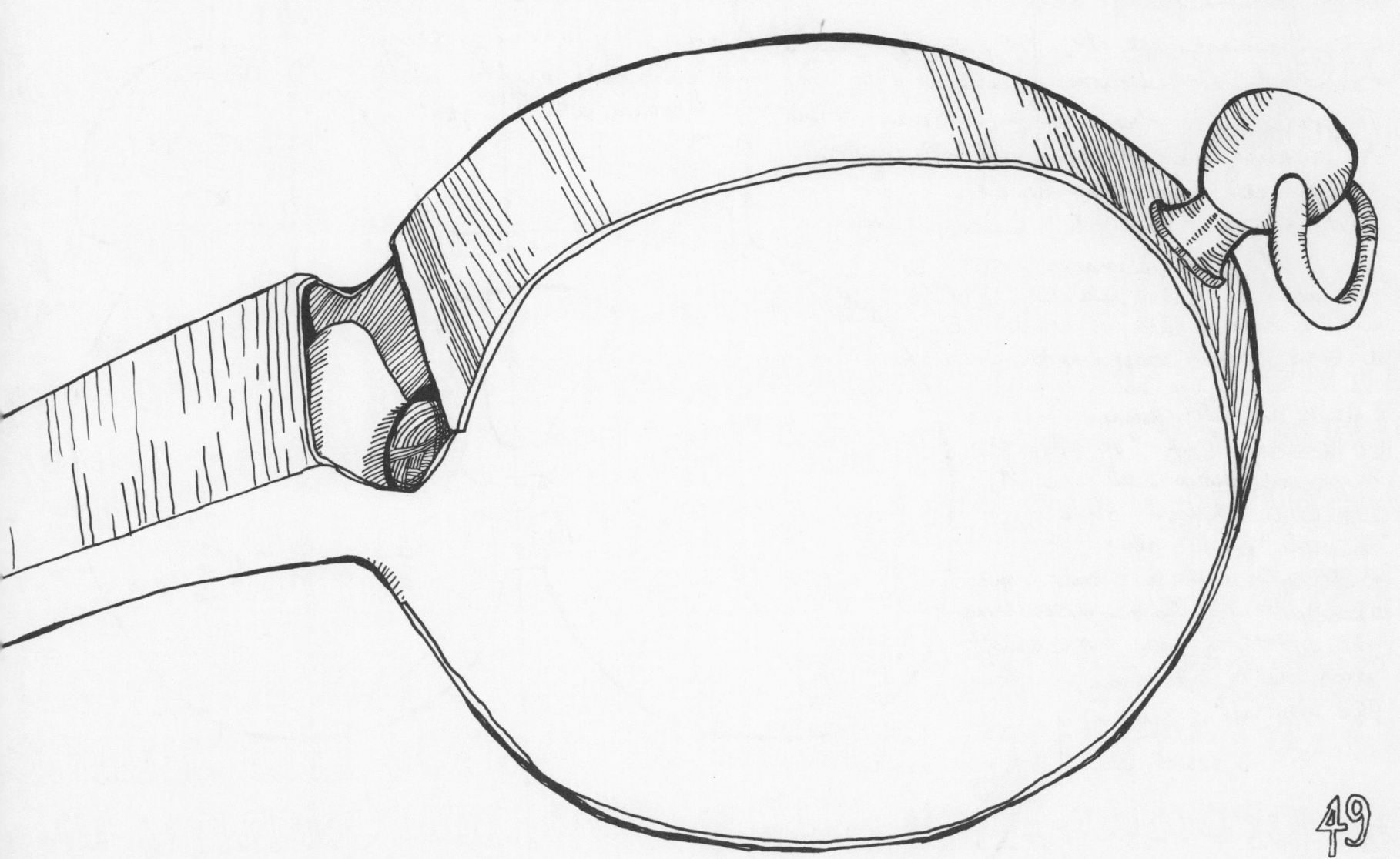

49

Indians in Peru created the whistling jar. From them the Spanish seem to have borrowed the idea and I have heard, though I've never seen one, that the Spanish make vessels for wine now on the same principle. Two vessels are connected by a passage, actually two passages, one clear, one at the top and a second, closer to the pot's bottom which, in this case has an added baffle. Water is poured in to about half-full and either by blowing into the spout or rocking the pot back and forth a whistle is produced. Two holes near the top on each side provide a place for air to escape. The baffle is not necessary but it does produce an added warble which, in the case of this pot made like a bird, seems most appropriate.

I know a potter named Bill who is making these. I've adapted his specifications to an ancient Peruvian example shown "complete" on the other page. Bill says that he's met some other potters who are discovering the whistling jar, some using some really interesting free-form and abstract shapes.

50

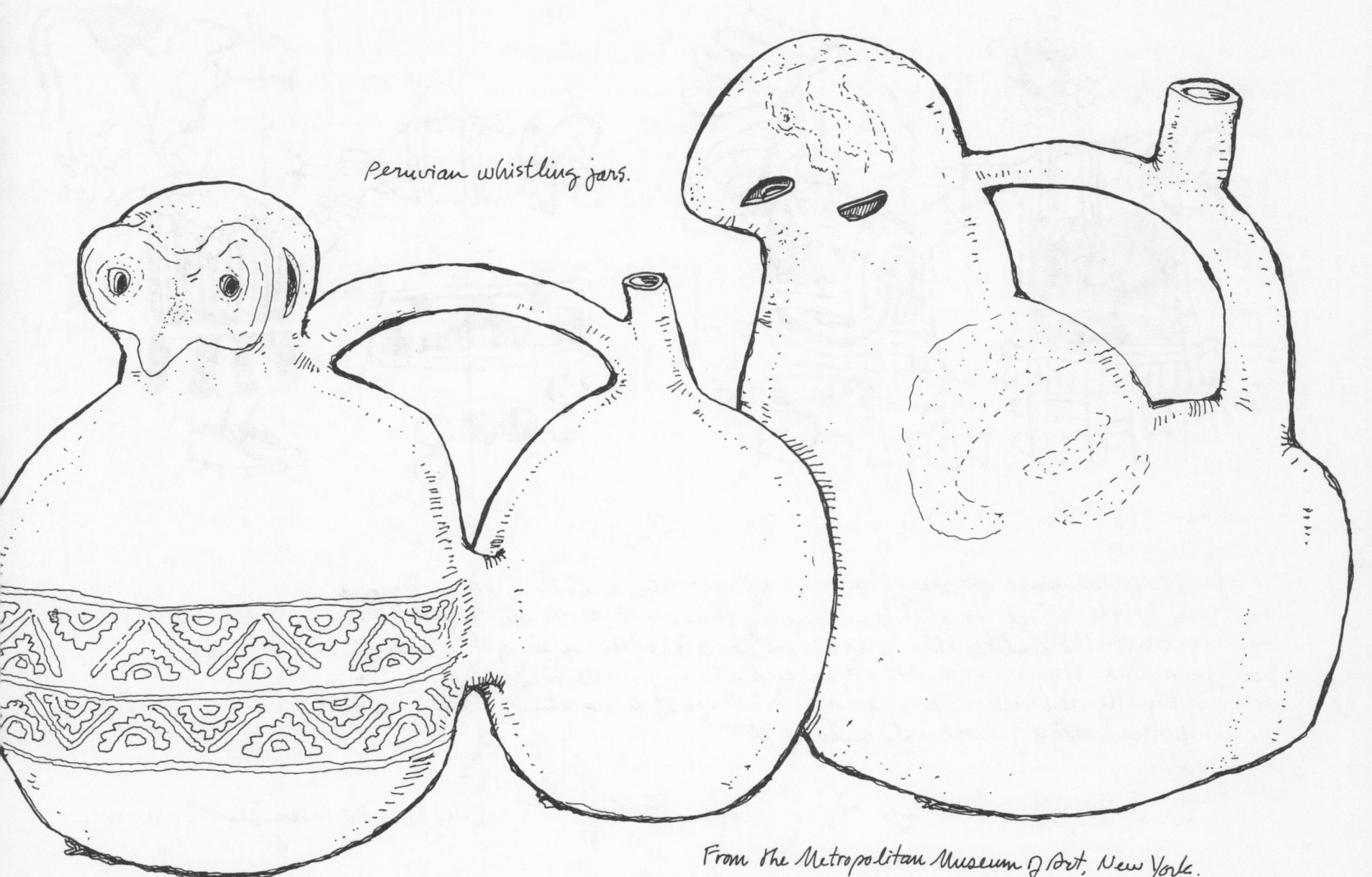

Peruvian whistling jars.

From the Metropolitan Museum of Art, New York.

51

These drawings are based on a Mayan tablet and illustrate a unique
whistle which is still found among some North American Indians. It is
constructed unlike other whistles for the air, after entering the passage,
meets a stopper near the upper end which diverts the air out of the
whistle and back in a second hole (the first being sharp-edged) by a
notched piece of wood attached to it.

Adapted from the Codex Becker. Vienna.

52

These little clay whistles are not especially melodic but they are charming. I drew them just for fun and because, being a great Batman fan, the one in the middle reminds me of the Penguin. Their proper name is cohuilotl or chilitli.

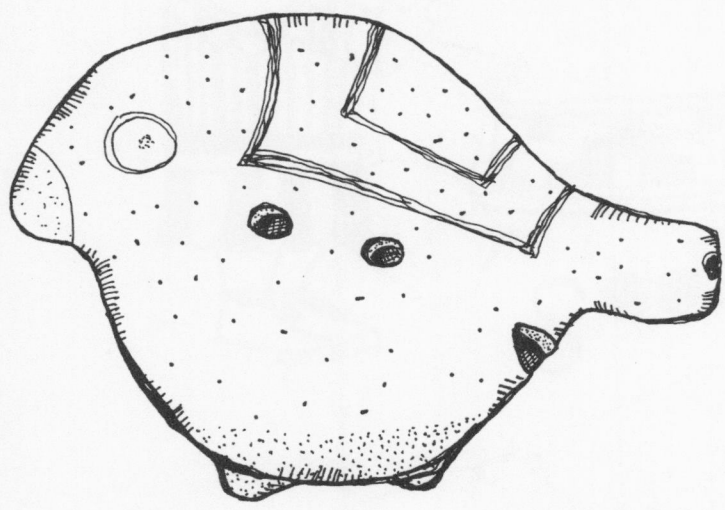

this little bird whistle is from Costa Rica.

These whistles, like most of the other pottery whistles I've drawn, can be easily made by coil-slab methods of pot-making.

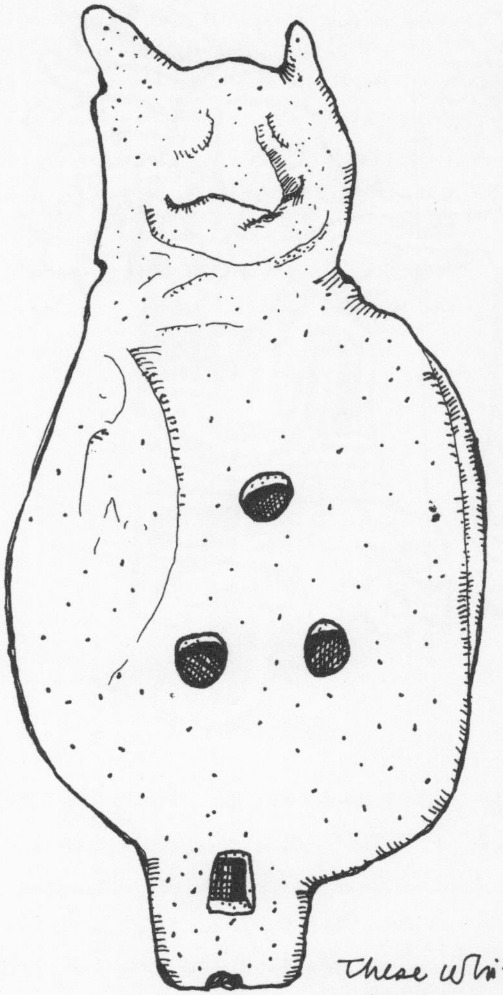

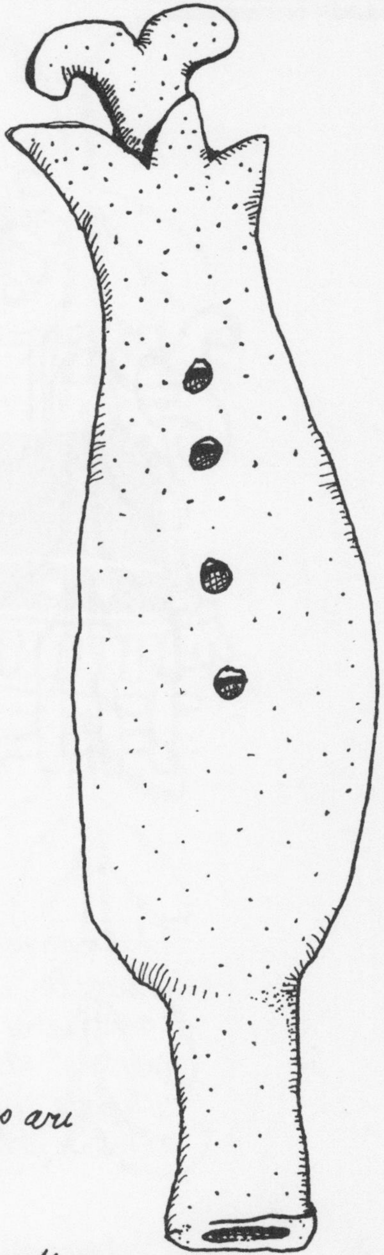

These whistles are Mexican.

All three of these whistles are in the Metropolitan Museum of Art, New York.

53

One of my favorite words is an old New Orleans creole word; Lagniappe (Lah-nyahp), meaning originally "a baker's dozen", something extra. Over the years it has become romanticized and means a bit more; a suprise, an unexpected kiss, a wind-fall, etc. One of the lagniappes of a walk in the country is the opportunity to make a willow whistle. Regardless of chronological age, it is a special, child-like joy. All it takes is a pen-knife and a piece of willow. And a little patience. If willow isn't handy, elderberry will do nicely. If you are lucky enough to be walking in the country with a special friend perhaps one lagniappe will lead to another.
The little poem on the opposite page teaches you all you need to know — about making a willow whistle.

How to make a willow whistle

First take a willow bough,
Smooth and round and dark,
And cut a little ring
Just through the outside bark.

Then tap and rap it gently
With many a tap and pound,
To loosen up the bark,
So it may turn round.

Slip the bark off carefully,
So that it will not break,
And cut away the inside part,
And then a mouthpiece make.

Now put the bark all nicely back,
And in a single minute
Just put it to your lips,
And blow the whistle in it.

                    Author unknown.

The border design is adapted from an early 19th Century folk-carving of a willow tree.

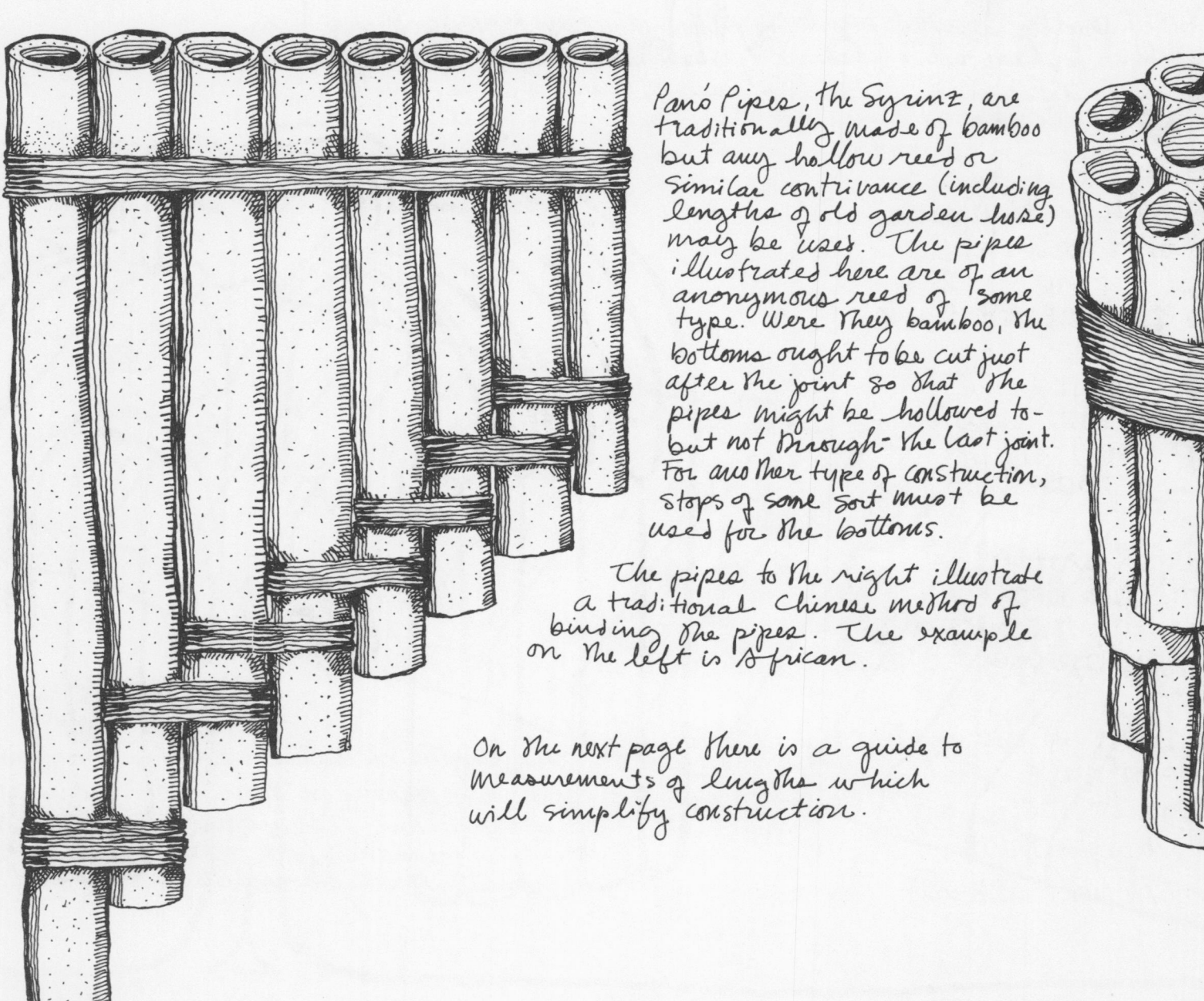

Pan's Pipes, the Syrinx, are
traditionally made of bamboo
but any hollow reed or
similar contrivance (including
lengths of old garden hose)
may be used. The pipes
illustrated here are of an
anonymous reed of some
type. Were they bamboo, the
bottoms ought to be cut just
after the joint so that the
pipes might be hollowed to-
but not through- the last joint.
For another type of construction,
stops of some sort must be
used for the bottoms.

The pipes to the right illustrate
a traditional Chinese method of
binding the pipes. The example
on the left is African.

On the next page there is a guide to
measurements of lengths which
will simplify construction.

It is hard to tell exactly at what point in history the Pan's Pipes first appear or where for there are evidences of such pipes in pre-historic China, among South American Indians, in ancient Greece, of course, which gave them their myth-inspired name, and they appeared in much of what is now Europe. In clusters, they are the ancestor of a host of musical instruments including the harmonica and it takes little imagination to turn one into a recorder.

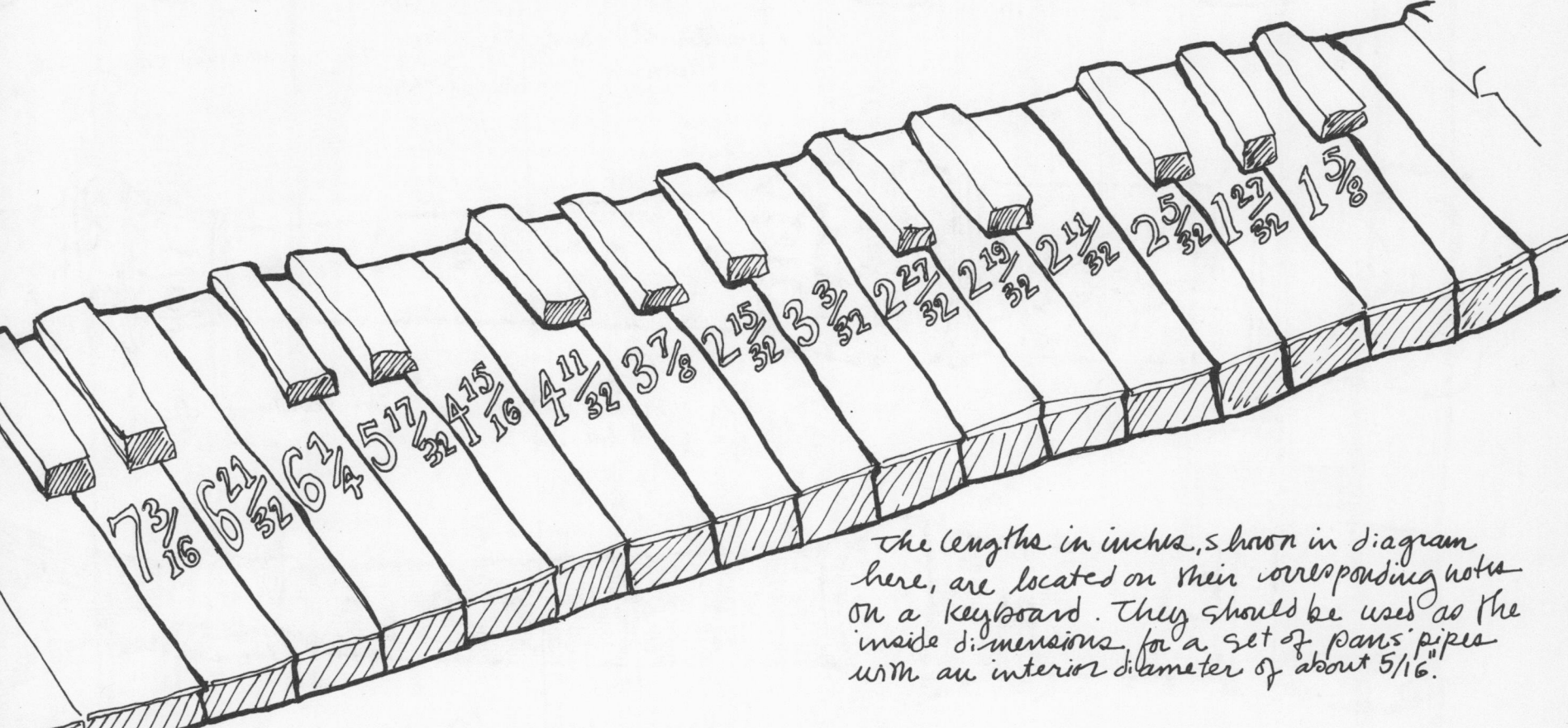

$7\frac{3}{16}$ $6\frac{21}{32}$ $6\frac{1}{4}$ $5\frac{17}{32}$ $4\frac{15}{16}$ $4\frac{11}{32}$ $3\frac{7}{8}$ $2\frac{15}{32}$ $3\frac{3}{32}$ $2\frac{27}{32}$ $2\frac{19}{32}$ $2\frac{11}{32}$ $2\frac{5}{32}$ $1\frac{27}{32}$ $1\frac{5}{8}$

the lengths in inches, shown in diagram here, are located on their corresponding notes on a keyboard. They should be used as the inside dimensions for a set of Pan's pipes with an interior diameter of about 5/16".

57

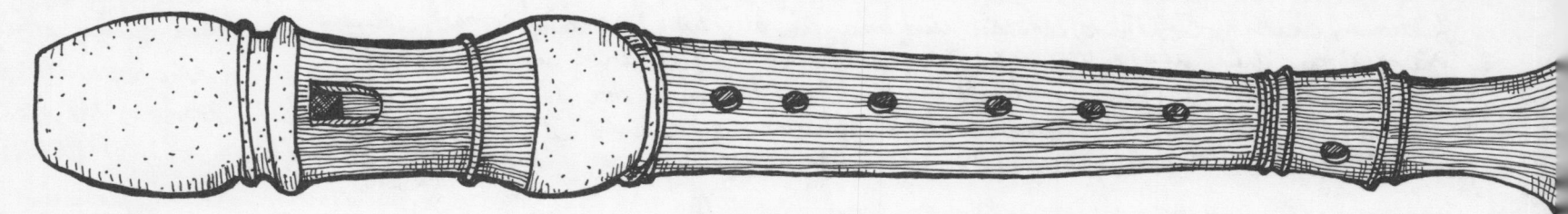

An Eighteenth Century Dutch Recorder. Wood and Ivory.
Soprano (Descant) in C.

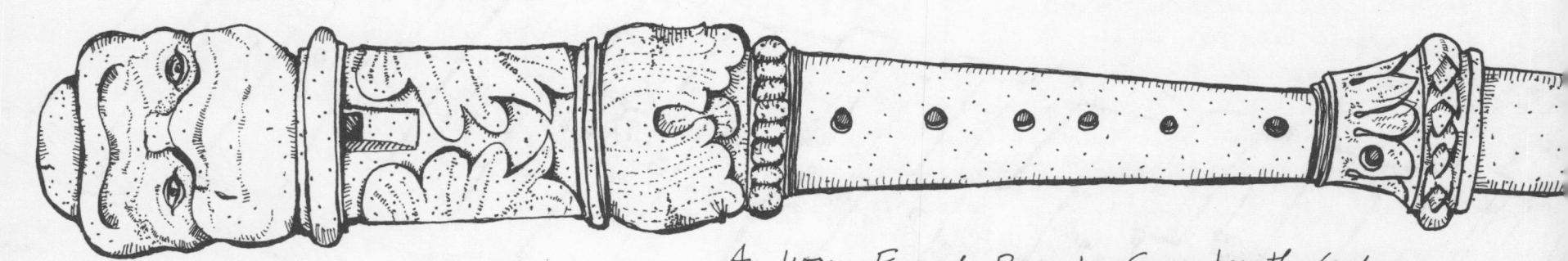

An Ivory French Recorder. Seventeenth Century.
Alto in F.

An Eighteenth Century German Recorder. Wood and Ivory.
Alto (treble) in F.

From the Metropolitan Museum of Art, New York.

I am shy to mention the word, bamboo, on a page opposite the three magnificent recorders from the Seventeenth and Eighteenth Centuries. Nor do I want to frighten anyone away from the instructions that follow by their thinking that those recorders are the ones I am suggesting just about anyone can make. They aren't. And I am not. So reason. I think it is appropriate to begin a section on SIMPLE flute and pipe making by showing an example of some of the best that can be done by hand, using simple tools, without an elaborate wood-working shop. However, the instruments I have concentrated on in this book are of a more primitive, folk-type and the instruments opposite are not for the beginner. The instructions that follow are.

Bamboo is the material I will use for these instruments. It is easy to work with; durable as well as flexible. It is easy to obtain, either naturally or from a supplier. If bought, you may have the option to choose between plain or tortoise which is actually "branded" or scorched with a iron. If you like you can make your own tortoise pattern the same way. Do that before you begin. For pipe-making, you will want the strongest bamboo you can find, free of cracks and holes, with as thin a wall as you can find. Measurements are given for inside dimensions.

These instructions are for three flutes, a treble pipe in the key of D, an alto pipe in A, and a tenor in the key of D - the octave below treble D; which is a good way to begin learning to make instruments like the ones on the facing page.

A Pipe in treble D.

Choose a piece of bamboo with the INSIDE diameter measuring at least 3/4" or a little more, not over an inch. Cut the length to 11½" which had better be too long. Remember, you can always trim it down but there's not too much you can do if you've cut more off that you ought. Chances are, you are going to have joints; try to cut the piece so that the joint is away from what will be your mouthpiece. Try to keep the joint about center. With an extension bit on a drill or an auger (no larger than ½") remove the inner part of the joint section. You should use a small round file to smooth it. You want as clear and straight and smooth an opening as possible.

59

Now, the mouthpiece. If you look at your clock or watch let this be your guide. Mark on the end of the bamboo, at the mouthpiece end, 6:30, 9:50 and 2:10. In other words, divide the end into three equal parts. Measuring down the pipe from the top end mark at 3/4". Now using a saw DELICATELY cut on a slant and remove all but 1/3 of that end section. On the other side of the pipe mark a point 1 1/4" and drill a 3/16" hole. This must be carefully shaped to an oval 3/16" high and 4/16" wide. A sloppy job here will cause a muddy tone to the finished pipe. With a pocket-knife, shave the bottom edge till it slants back at a 45° angle. The inside is not cut, it has to keep its sharp edge. Be careful not to affect the size of the window by this sill.

Form the passage — the ridge on the inner side of the pipe 1/20" deep, squared at the sides and placed from the window to the end of the mouthpiece. Cut a tiny groove for a buffer.

I have heard of cork being used to fit the mouthpiece. A well-trimmed piece of soft wood would be better. But it should be shaped for a good fit; so that a slit appears between the passage and the wood (or cork) shave off a thin edge. When the piece is in, it should not show below the window.

With any luck at all, you should hear your first clear note on the pipe. By using a piano, check the pitch and shorten slightly for any correction. At this point it is between you and your ear and the pipe. All pipes vary so no measurements can help here.

Measure from the bottom of the pipe to the center of the window. Divide this by four and, starting at the bottom end of the pipe, this is where you place your first hole. From 2 1/4" from the center of the window place the sixth hole. The six holes will be equally spaced between these two points. But check each hole with the piano before you place the next one. On the other side of the pipe, directly behind the sixth hole, place the thumb hole.

An alto pipe in the key of A.

Length-wise and pitch-wise this pipe is half-way between the other two pipes.

The interior diameter of the bamboo should be between 7/8" to 1¼". Start with a 16" length of bamboo. Everything is identical to making the treble pipe _except_ the dimensions. The window is a little larger and 1½" from the top to center. Make the window 5/16" x ¼". Tune the first note the same as before and shorten to adjust the pitch.

For the finger holes measure ¼ distance from the window's center to the pipe's bottom. At that point mark the first note. From 3¾" from the center of the window mark the sixth. A space of at least 1½" to 2" must be left between the third and fourth holes of this pipe. Otherwise, mark the remaining holes in threes convenient for the fingers.

The tenor pipe.

Choose a bamboo-piece with inside diameter between 1⅛" to 1½". Work with a 22" length this time. For the first cut at the mouth-piece allow a full inch instead of ¾" as before. Place the window 1½" down and make it 3/8" x 3/8". For the holes, measure ¼ of distance from the bottom to the center of the window. Mark the first ¼ up and add 1" for the first hole. The sixth hole is placed at 6¾" from the center of the window. The thumb-hole may be ¾" higher. The holes must be in two groups of three, allowing about an inch between each except, of course, between the third and fourth holes which needs a somewhat larger gap.

The reed pipes on the frontispiece are made by this same procedure except they have no finger-holes. Each pipe plays only one note. By joining them together, raft-like, an instrument is created with as wide a range   can be put together and held in the hands.

61

Hole Diameter

C Fife	2 1/64"	11/64"	1/4"	1/4"	7/32"	7/32"	11/64"
B Flat Fife	2 1/64"	5/32"	7/32"	13/64"	1/8"	11/64"	5/32"

Hole Distance

C Fife	4 17/32"	5 19/32"	6 37/64"	7 31/64"	8 27/64"	9 3/8"	11 39/64"
B Flat Fife	5 19/32"	6 37/64"	7 39/64"	8 15/32"	9 3/8"	10 9/32"	12 5/64"

Hole Distance

7/16"

13" C FIFE

14 1/4" B FLAT FIFE

These tables detail dimensions for building two fifes,
one in the key of C the other in B Flat. The distance
measurements start at the center of the embochure
each time. The interior diameter is the same for both fifes.

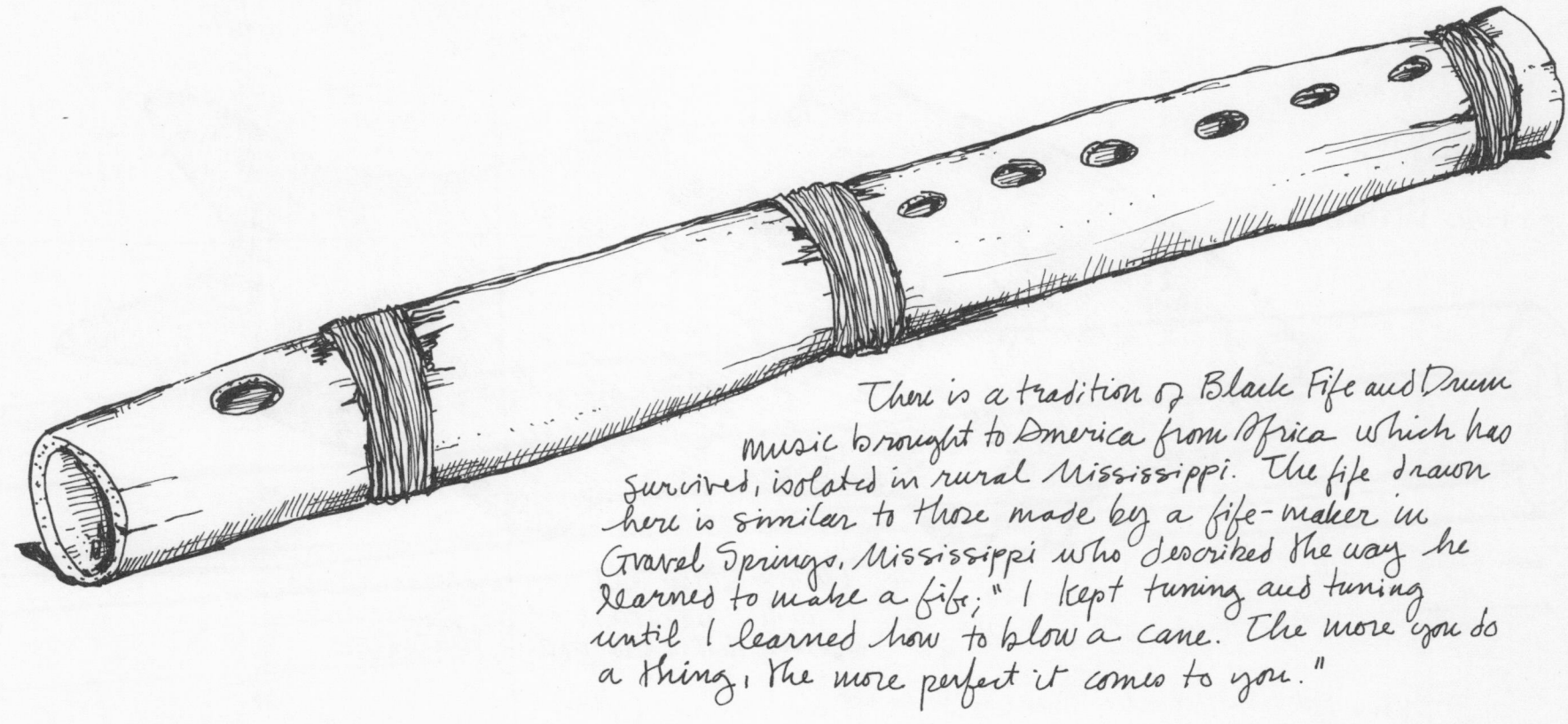

There is a tradition of Black Fife and Drum
music brought to America from Africa which has
survived, isolated in rural Mississippi. The fife drawn
here is similar to those made by a fife-maker in
Gravel Springs, Mississippi who described the way he
learned to make a fife; " I kept tuning and tuning
until I learned how to blow a cane. The more you do
a thing, the more perfect it comes to you."

63

Carol has this wonderful Ocarina
from Mexico. You can play a pretty
good tune on it. The fish's mouth
is the mouthpiece.

This is pottery and was made in Oxaca.
It is that beautiful black, almost like
silk, that their pottery is there.

The Ocarina probably developed from an ancient Chinese globe-shaped flute.
which was molded on eggs; a chicken's for the inside, maybe a goose egg
for the outside. But a man named Donati, in Southern Italy is given
credit for inventing the modern ocarina, in the 1860's.

By varying sizes, the instruments can be made in sets, from treble to bass.
In fact, there was great popularity in Europe in the last century for
ocarina orchestras.

In America, the ocarina has often been
called the sweet potatoe because it resembles
one.

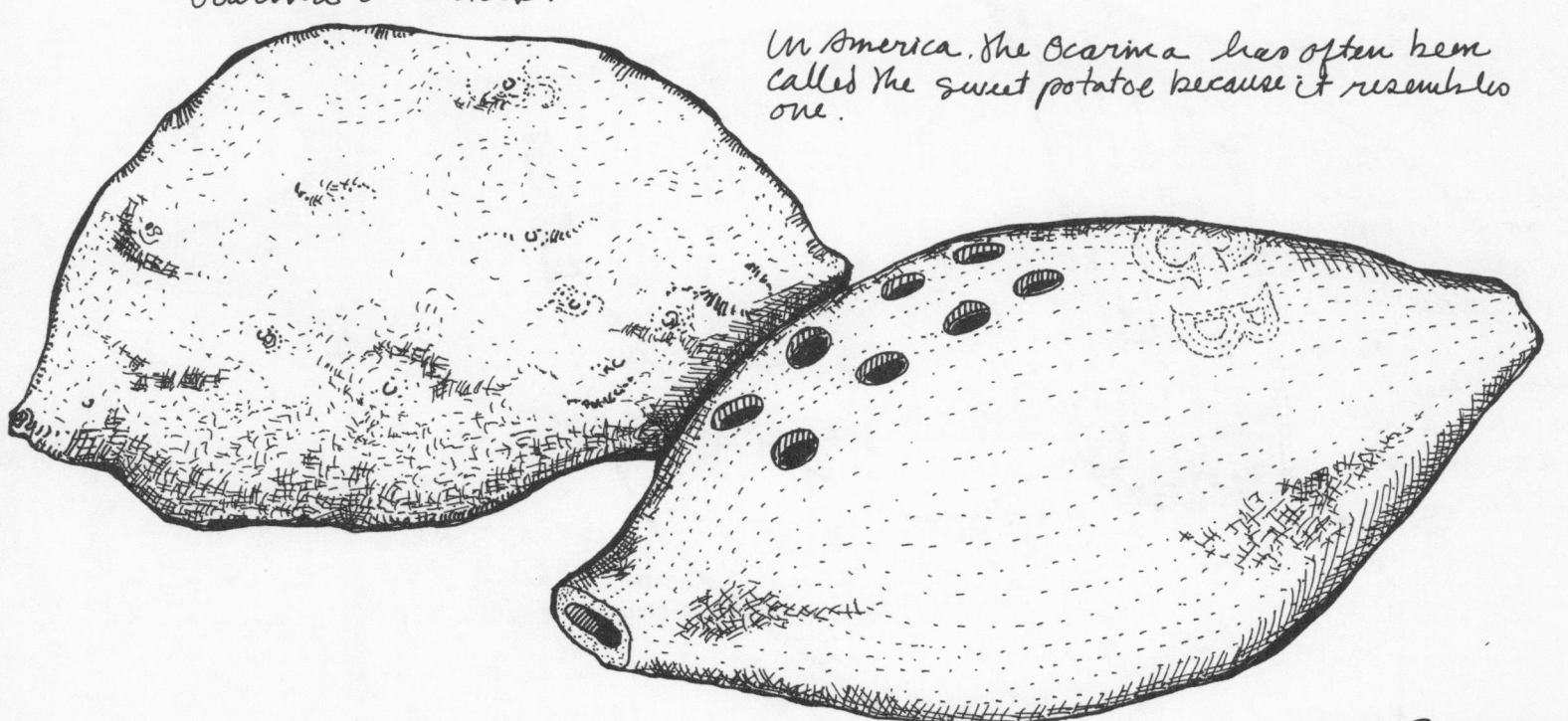

My friend Pam owns this
ocarina, a "real" sweet potatoe,
made of red clay. She thinks it
was homemade in Tennessee.

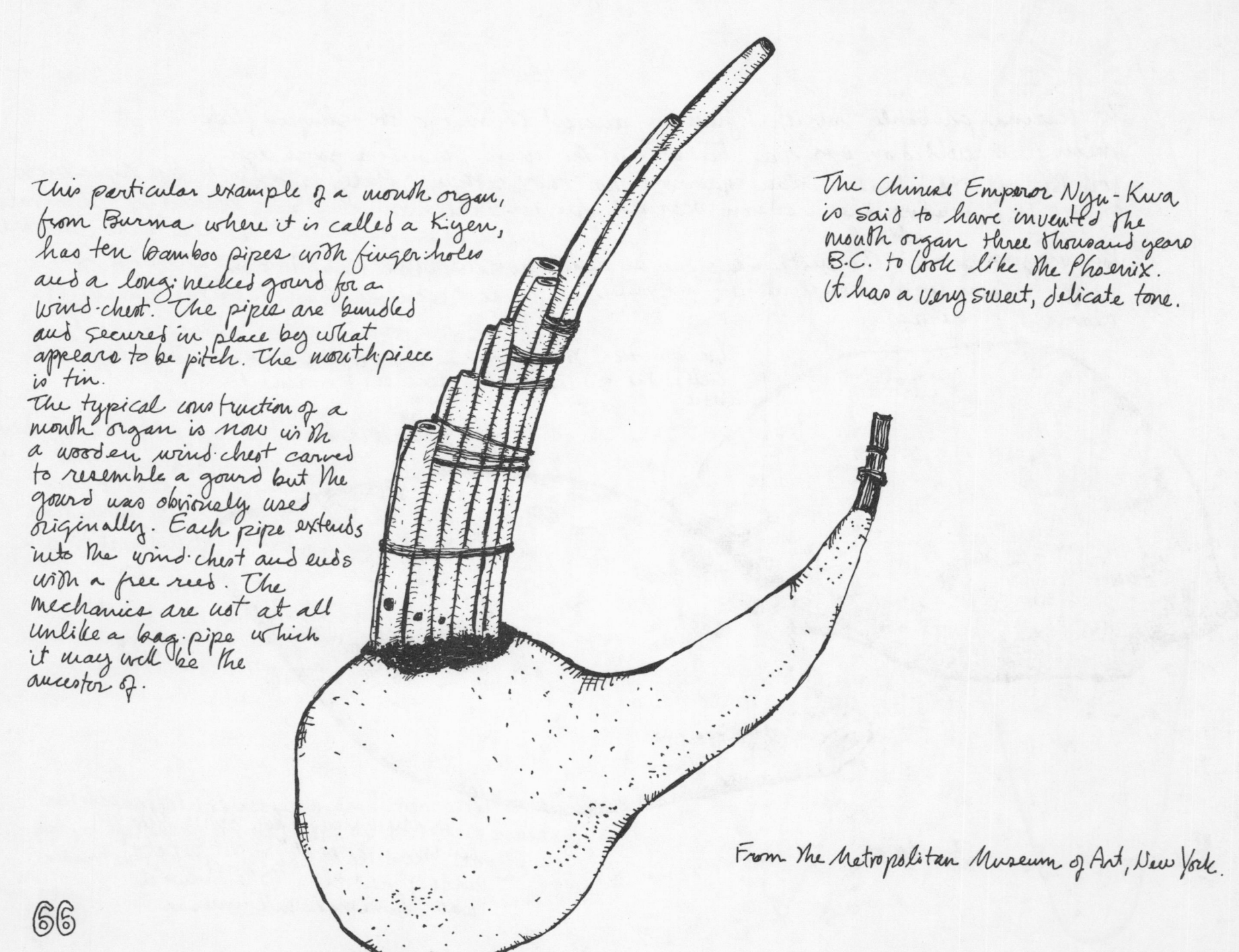

This particular example of a mouth organ, from Burma where it is called a Kyen, has ten bamboo pipes with finger-holes and a long-necked gourd for a wind-chest. The pipes are bundled and secured in place by what appears to be pitch. The mouthpiece is tin.

The typical construction of a mouth organ is now with a wooden wind-chest carved to resemble a gourd but the gourd was obviously used originally. Each pipe extends into the wind-chest and ends with a free reed. The mechanics are not at all unlike a bag-pipe which it may well be the ancestor of.

The Chinese Emperor Nyu-Kwa is said to have invented the mouth organ three thousand years B.C. to look like the Phoenix. It has a very sweet, delicate tone.

From the Metropolitan Museum of Art, New York.

66

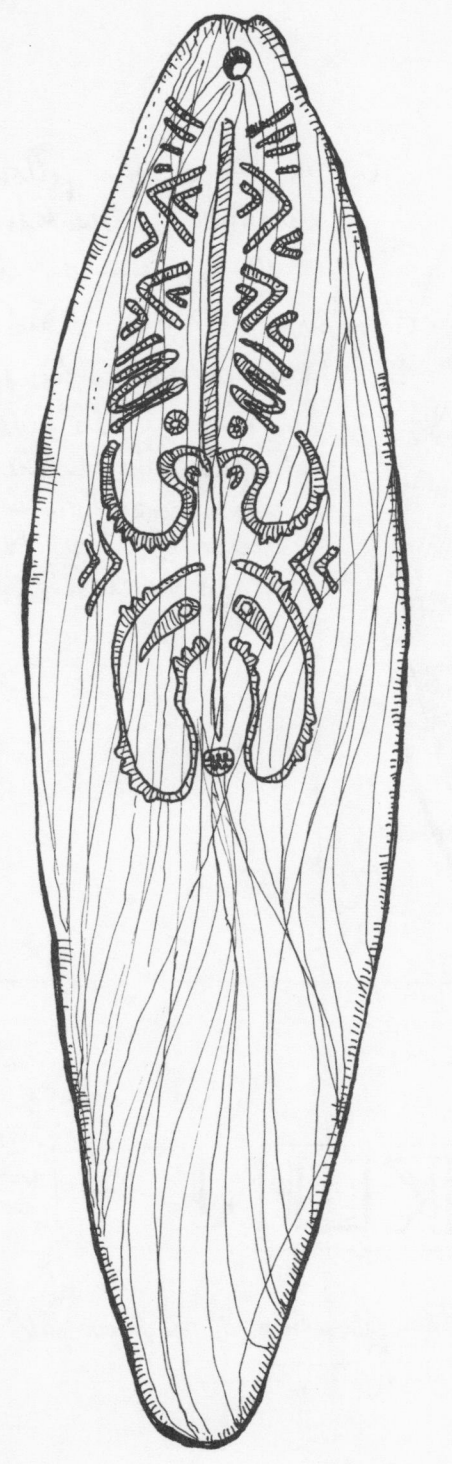

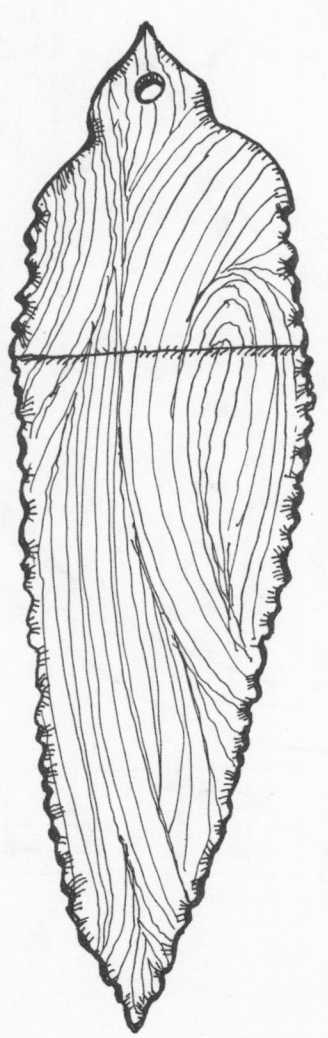

Any child who has played with the paper birds or airplanes on a string bought at carnivals or twirled a ruler in the air has discovered the bull-roarer. It was one of man's first musical instrument discoveries and exists today, in one form or other, over the earth. In Malay it is used to chase elephants out of fields.

The bull-roarer is essentially a flat, wooden blade, roughly thinner at the edges, and oval-shaped. It is attached to a cord and propelled over the head. The only variation in sound is acheived by a bull-roarer of a different size.

Primitive man gave it special magical significance, believing that it contained within it or called-forth the voice of his ancestors.

The bull-roarers here are from the Metropolitan Museum of Art, New York. The one on the left is from New Guinea and the one on the right, Australia.

67

Benjamin Franklin invented
or perfected a musical
instrument already
existing in some form
which he called the
Armonica. In so
doing Franklin added
to history the first
musical instrument
invented by an
American.

On the pages that follow is
a narrative in Franklin's
own words, from a letter
to an Italian friend while
Franklin was in London,
describing his invention.
The letter tells the
friend — and us —
precisely how to build
the Armonica.

BENJAMIN FRANKLIN

68

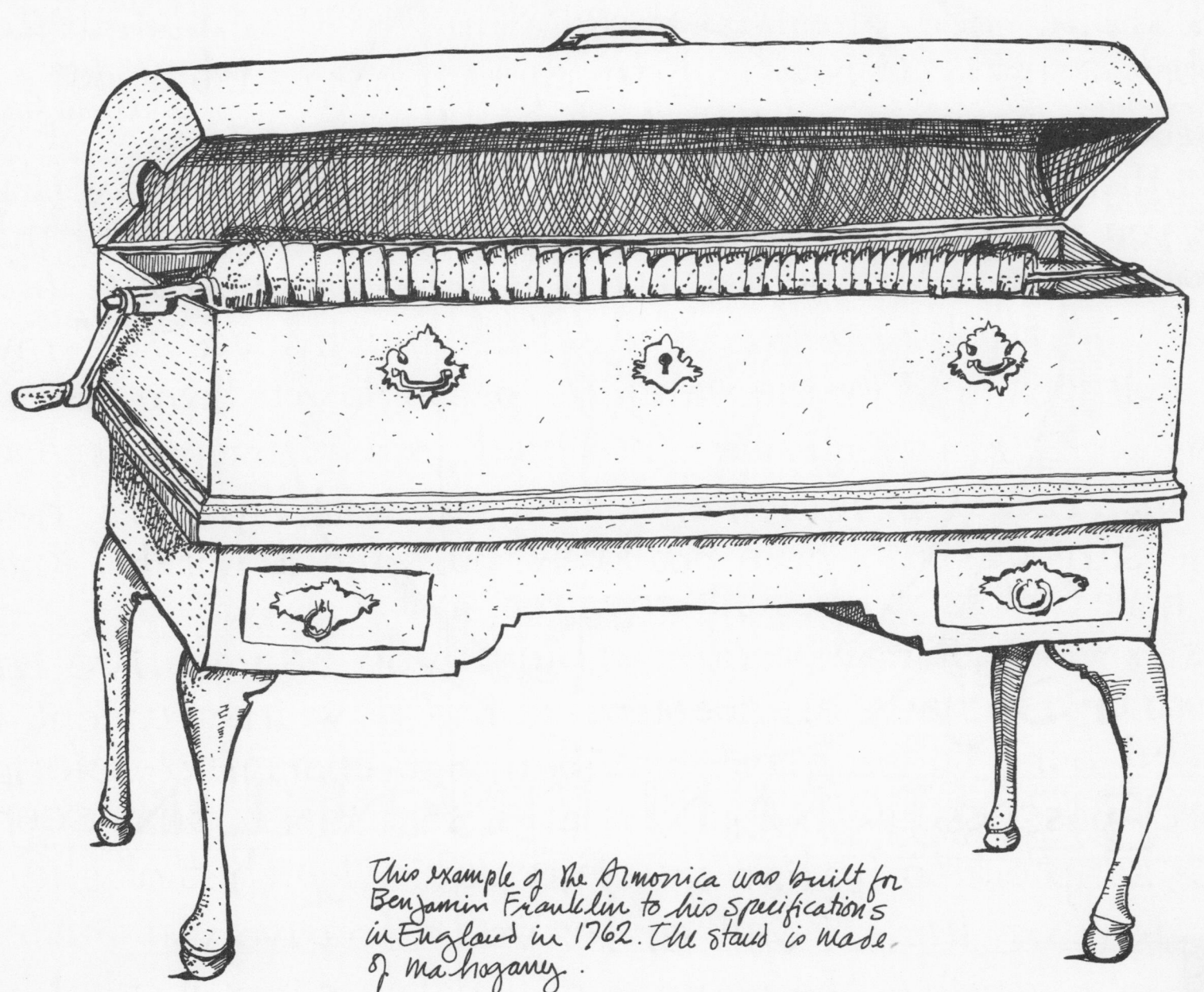

This example of the Armonica was built for Benjamin Franklin to his specifications in England in 1762. The stand is made of mahogany.

69

London, July 13, 1763

Reverend Sir: I once promised myself the pleasure of seeing you at Turin; but as that is not now likely to happen, being just about returning to my native country, America, I sit down to take leave of you (among others of my European friends that I cannot see) by writing.

I thank you for the honourable mention you have so frequently made of me in your letters to Mr. Collinson and others; for the generous defence you undertook and executed with so much success, of my electrical opinions; and for the valuable present you have made me of your new work, from which I have received great information and pleasure. I wish I could in return entertain you with anything new of mine on the subject; but I have not lately pursued it. Nor do I know of anyone here that is at present engaged in it.

Perhaps, however, it may be agreeable to you, as you live in a musical country, to have an account of the new instrument lately added here to the great number that charming science was before possessed of. As it is an instrument that seems peculiarly adapted to Italian music, especially that of the soft and plaintive kind, I will endeavour to give you such a description of it, and of the manner of constructing it, that you or any of your friends may be enabled to imitate it, if you incline so to do, without being at the expense and trouble of the many experiments I have made in endeavouring to bring it to its present perfection.

You have doubtless heard the sweet tone that is drawn from a drinking glass by passing a wet finger round its brim. One Mr. Puckeridge, a gentleman from Ireland, was the first who thought of playing tunes, formed of these tones. He collected a number of glasses of different sizes, fixed them near each other on a table, and tuned them by putting into them water more or less, as each note required. The tones were brought out by passing his fingers round their brims. He was unfortunately burned here, with his instrument, in a fire which consumed the house he lived in. Mr. E. Delaval, a most ingenious member of our Royal Society, made one in imitation of it, with a better choice and form of glasses, which was the first

I saw or heard. Being charmed by the sweetness of its tones, & the music he produced from it, I wished only to see the glasses disposed in a more convenient form, and brought together in a narrower compass, so as to admit of a greater number of tones, and all within reach of hand to a person sitting before the instrument, which I accomplished, after various intermediate trials and less commodiou forms, both of glasses and construction, in the following manner.

The glasses are blown as near as possible in the form of hemispheres having each an open neck or socket in the middle. The thickness of the glass near the brim about a tenth of an inch, or hardly quite s much, but thicker as it comes nearer the neck, which in the largest glasses is about an inch deep, and an inch and half wide within, these dimensions lessening, as the glasses themselves diminish in size, except that the neck of the smallest ought not to be shorter than half an inch. The largest glass is nine inches diameter, & the smallest three inches. Between these two are twenty-three different sizes, differing from each other a quarter of an inch in diameter. To make a single instrument there shoud be at least si glasses blown of each size; and out of this number one may probably pick thirty-seven glasses (which are sufficient for thr octaves with all the semi-tones) that will be each either the note one wants or a little sharper than that note, and all fitting so well into each other as to tapper pretty regularly from the largest to the smallest. It is true there are not thirty-seven sizes, but it often happens that two of the same size differ a note or half-note in tone, by reason of a difference in thickness, and these may be placed one in the other without sensibly hurting the regularity of the taper form.

The glasses being chosen, and every one marked with a diamond the note you intend it for, they are to be tuned by diminshing the thickness of those that are too sharp. This is done by grinding them round from the neck towards the brim, the breadth of one or two inches, as may be required; often trying the glass by a well-tuned harpsicord, comparing the tone drawn from the glass by your finger with the note you want, as sounded by that string of the harpsicord. When you come nearer the matter, be careful to wipe the glass clean and dry before each trial, because the tone is something flatter when the glass is wet than it will be when dry; and grinding a very little between each trial, you will thereby tune to great exactness. The more care is necessary in this because, if you go below your required tone, there is no sharpening it again but by grinding somewhat off the brim, which will afterwards require polishing and thus increase the trouble.

The glasses being thus tuned, you are to be provided with a case for them, and a spindle on which they are to be fixed. My case is about three feet long, eleven inches every way wide within at the biggest end, and five inches at the smallest end; for it tapers all the way, to adapt it better to the conical figure of the set of glasses. This case opens in the middle of its height, & the upper part turns up by hinges fixed behind. The spindle, which is of hard iron, lies horizontally from end to end of the box within, exactly in the middle, and is made to turn on brass gudgeons at each end. It is round, an inch diameter at the thickest end, and tapering to a quarter of an inch at the smallest. A square shank comes from its thickest end through the box, on which shank a wheel is fixed by a screw. This wheel serves as a fly to make the motion equable, when the spindle, with the glasses, is turned by the foot like a

Spinning-wheel. My wheel is of mahogany, eighteen inches diameter, and pretty thick, so as to conceal near it circumference about twenty-five pounds of lead. An ivory pin is fixed in the face of this wheel, and about four inches from the axis. Over the neck of this pin is put the loop of the string that comes up from the moveable step to give it motion. The case stands on a neat frame with four legs.

To fix the glasses on the spindle, a cork is first to be fitted in each neck pretty tight, and projecting a little without the neck, that the neck of one may not touch the inside of another when put together, for that would make a jarring. These corks are to be perforated with holes of different diameters, so as to suit that part of the spindle on which they are to be fixed. When a glass is put on, by holding it stiffly between both hands, while another turns the spindle, it may be gradually brought to its place. But care must be taken that the hole be not too small, lest, in forcing it up, the neck should split; nor too large, lest the glass, not being firmly fixed, should turn or move on the spindle, so as to touch and jar against its neighbouring glass. The glasses thus are placed one in another. the largest on the biggest end of the spindle, which is to the left hand; the neck of this glass is towards the wheel, and the next goes into it in the same position, only about an inch of its brim appearing beyond the brim of the first; thus proceeding, every glass when fixed shows about an inch of its brim (or three-quarters of an inch, or half an inch, as they grow smaller) beyond the brim of the glass that contains it; and it is from these exposed parts of each glass that the tone is drawn, by laying a finger upon one of them as the spindle and glasses turn round.

My largest glass is G, a little below the reach of a common voice, and my highest G. including three complete octaves. To distinguish the glasses the more readily to the eye, I have painted the apparent parts of the glasses within side, every semi-tone white, and the other notes of the octave with the seven prismatic colours, viz., C, red; D, orange; E, yellow; F, green; G, blue; A, indigo; B, purple; and C, red again; so that glasses of the same colour (the white excepted) are always octaves to each other.

This instrument is played upon, by sitting before the middle of the set of glasses as before the keys of a harpsicord, turning them with the foot, and wetting them now and then with a sponge and clean water. The fingers should be first a little soaked in water, & quite free from all greasiness; a little fine chalk upon them is sometimes useful, to make them catch the glass and bring out the tone more readily. Both hands are used, by which means different parts are played together. Observe, that the tones are best drawn out when the glasses turn *from* the ends of the fingers, not when they turn *to* them.

The advantages of this instrument are that its tones are incomparably sweet beyond those of any other; that they may be swelled and softened at pleasure by stronger or weaker pressures of the finger, and continued to any length; and that the instrument, being once well tuned, never again wants tuning.

In honour of your musical language, I have borrowed from it the name of this instrument, calling it the Armonica.

Benj. Franklin

drum¹, n. Musical instrument sounded by striking & made of hollow cylinder or hemisphere with parchment stretched over opening(s) (bass, tenor, big, KETTLE, &c., d.); (Zool.) natural organ giving resonance, as howling monkey's hyoid bone; sound (as) of d., esp. bittern's cry; player of d., drumme cylindrical structure (d. of ear,

This simple frame drum, stretched over the outside of the hoop, is decorated with a totemic raven. It is from the Chilkat Indians, Nushagak Bay, Alaska.

From the Metropolitan Museum of Art, New York.

79

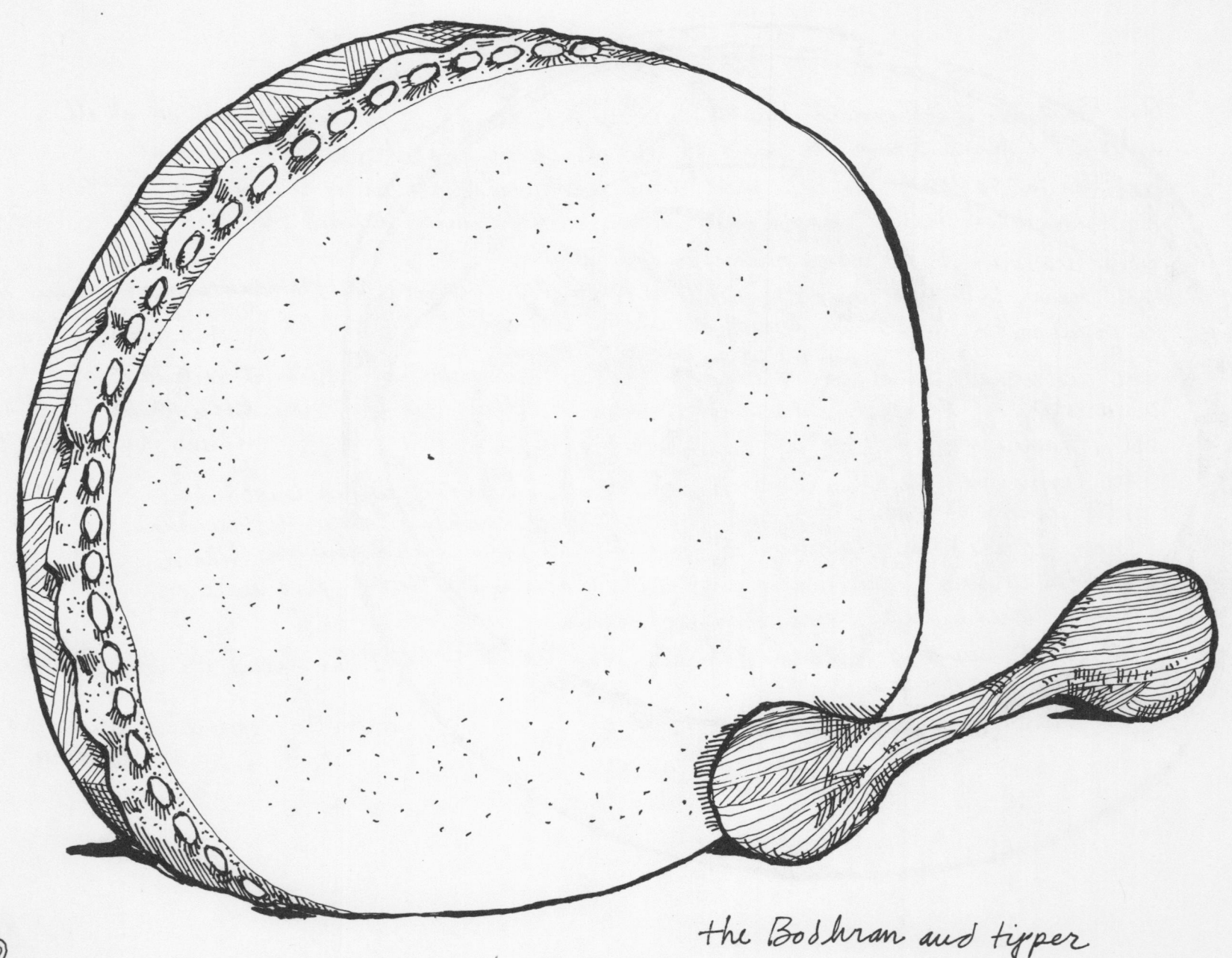

the Bodhran and tipper

80

The Bodhran (pronounced bow-Rawn) is a frame drum, at first glance not at all unlike the frame drum on page 94. It has been a part of Irish musical tradition for so long that its exact time and place of origin is questionable. There is a suggestion that it may have been brought into Ireland by Vikings who acquired it on wanderings in the East.

Like many folk instruments, the bodhran is enjoying a tremendous revival in popularity, both in America and in Ireland.

The instrument is often referred to as a tambourine which it certainly is a variety of however it rarely has rattles and is, more often than not, played with a stick, called a "tipper".

The tipper is usually carved from ash or hickory and is knobbed at both ends. Its usual size is about eight inches long. When the tipper is used for playing. it is held in the hand much like a pencil is held with the palm-side facing the body and more or less turned away from the bodhran.

When the hand is used for playing, the back side of the hand strikes the drum.

Bodhran-making has its own peculiar method of preparing a skin. I have heard stories about the skin of a greyhound being used but I'd rather not even think about that. Goat skin is found often enough to be considered the norm. The process is as follows:

The goat carcass is slit up from the tail on the underside for several inches and then around the hind legs. The next slit is up the middle to the head. The skin immediately above the front legs is then carefully slit.

With a sharp knife the skin is "punched" away from the flesh and after some is free all around the rest can be pulled away from the tail upwards. The hide is then rubbed with lime against the grain of hair so that it gets in evenly underneath. Fold the skin over once and then roll it into a bundle, flesh-side out. It is tied securely and buried for nine days. It is then taken out, any remaining hair or flesh is removed and the skin is left in a stream for three days after which time it is stretched tightly to a door.

The hoop is made of green ash and is usually about 16 inches in diameter. Three people are needed to complete the bodhran; two people stretch the skin over the hoop while the third tacks it in place. The completed drum is left near an open fire overnight to cure and then rubbed with resin.

Two wires are attached on the inside of the hoop, criss-crossed, to give the player something to hold the bodhran by.

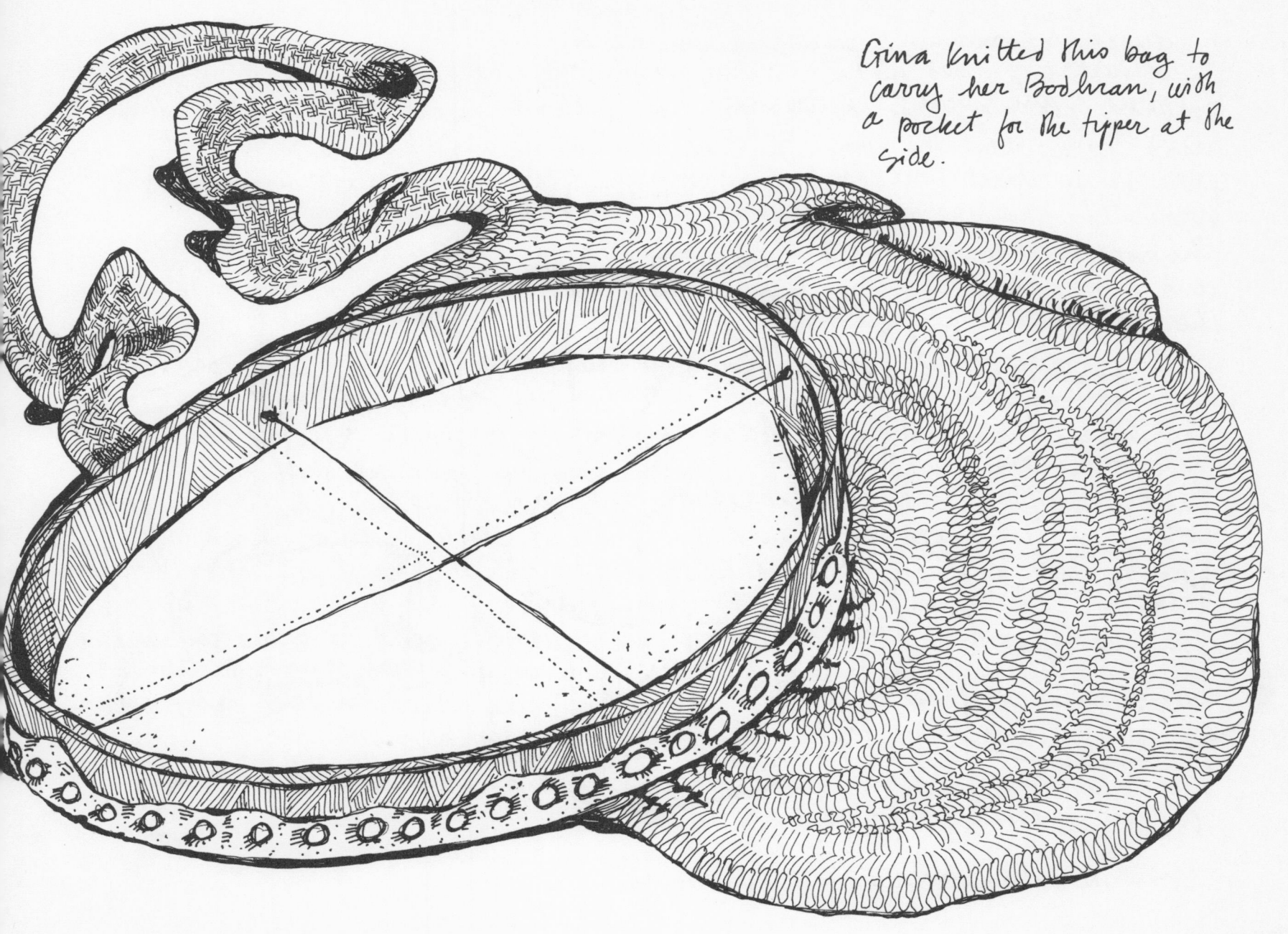

Gina knitted this bag to carry her Bodhran, with a pocket for the tipper at the side.

83

The Saing Waing Ah-Pwe is a Burmese theatrical ensemble consisting of pantomime dancers and an orchestra of tuned metal drums, much like the steel drum bands of The Americas.

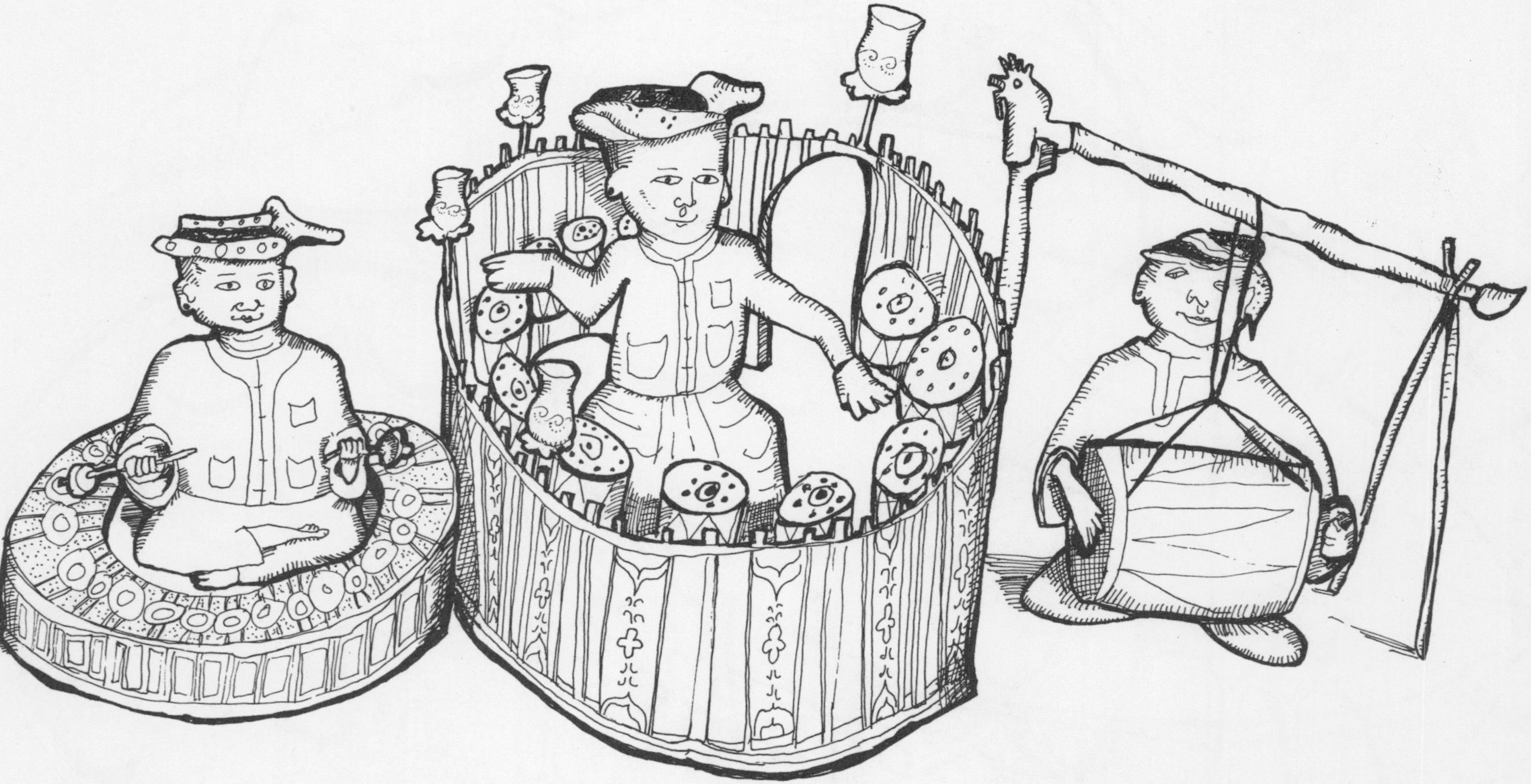

From The Metropolitan Museum of Art, New York.

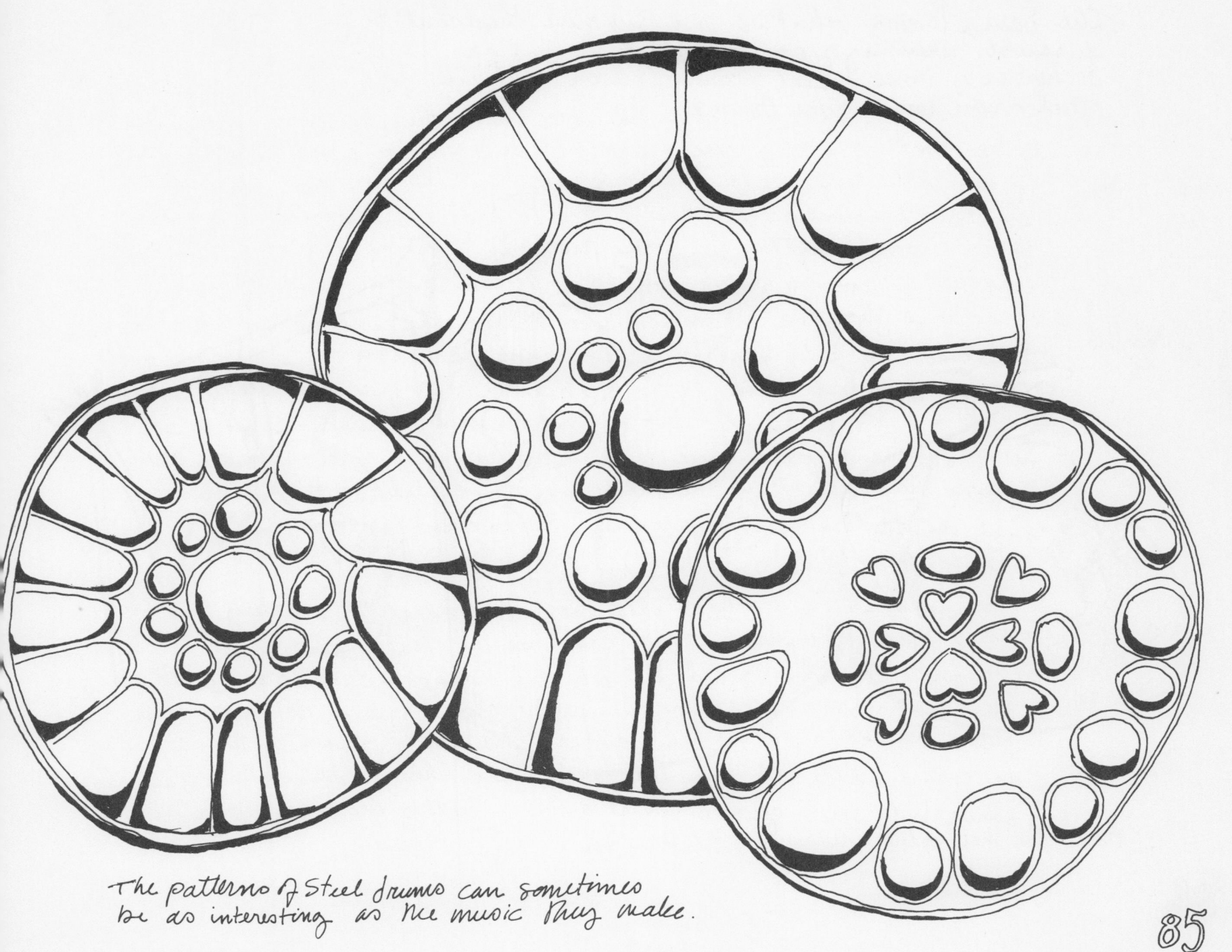

The patterns of steel drums can sometimes
be as interesting as the music they make.

85

Steel Drums must be one of the more facinating musical instruments of the Americas. They come from Trinidad with its colorful blendings of cultures and people. The story goes that local people discovered empty oil drums on the beaches left behind by American military forces during World War II. The people of Trinidad already had a tradition of bamboo sticks tuned for music making and when it was discovered that the drums discarded by the Americans were musical, or could be, the steel drum was born.

Making a steel drum is not easy. It requires a unique blend of a good ear for pitch and a high tolerance for noise. This is not an instrument for anyone to make anywhere. You need an open space with few or no neighbours or a metal-working shop. But the tools are simple and the actual process is not complicated.

Steel drums are pounded into tune. They are not delicately turned and shaped. They are a far cry from the willow whistle.

The first step is to "sink" the top of a large metal drum with a sledge hammer, creating a gently-sloped basin not more than four inches deep at the center. Patterns, such as on page 85, are marked on the top. The areas are then divided with a nail punch into small grooves. These are gradually increased with a large metal wedge. The drum is cut apart from the barrel, about six to ten inches down from the top.   Working from the bottom side, each tone area is tapped up so that, from the top, it is convex. Over a bon-fire or with a torch the drums are tempered. Heated and then immediately douced with water, the drum is ready for tuning. The tolerance for constant pounding has been valuable up to this point. Now the good ear is essential. Each tone area must be gently tapped into tune with its corresponding note on a piano or harmonica.

A full steel orchestra consists of "ping pong" pans with twenty-five notes in a chromatic scale, a second section consisting of pans with fourteen notes - in approximately alto range, and cello and guitar pans which are roughly bass and tenor.

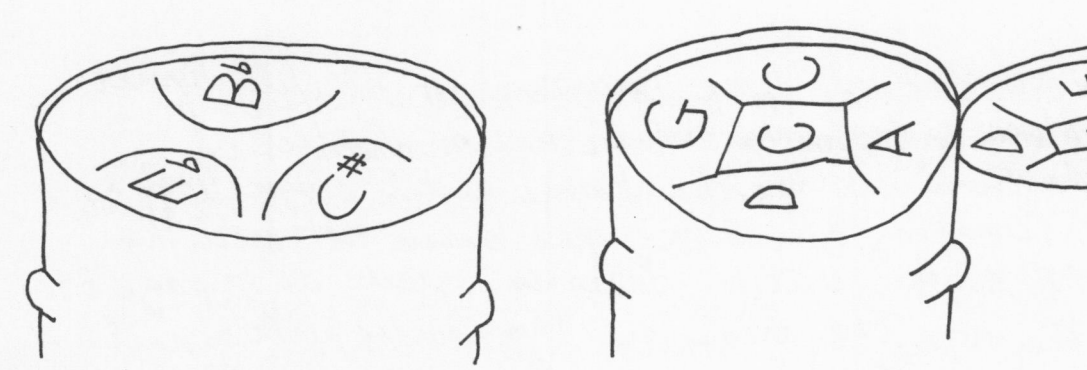

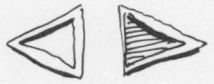

Of the many musical instruments commonly considered to be African in origin there is one that is most certainly African; the Sansa or Kafir-piano, sometimes called a Thumb-piano or a Thumb xylophone. Wherever the Sansa appears throughout the world it does so only through direct contact with Africa.

The xylophone is often mistaken for an instrument that originated in Africa. Actually, it came from Indonesia. In its purest form - a single slab of wood struck to produce a sound - the xylophone is an indication of the origin of the Sansa. It produces a sound that quietly and delicately immitates the xylophone.

The construction of the Sansa is simple. Tongs are fastened to a board - sometimes with, sometimes without a resonator. They are tuned by length and played by plucking them with the thumb.

On the following pages are examples of the sansa from Africa and instructions for making a Thumb-piano at home.

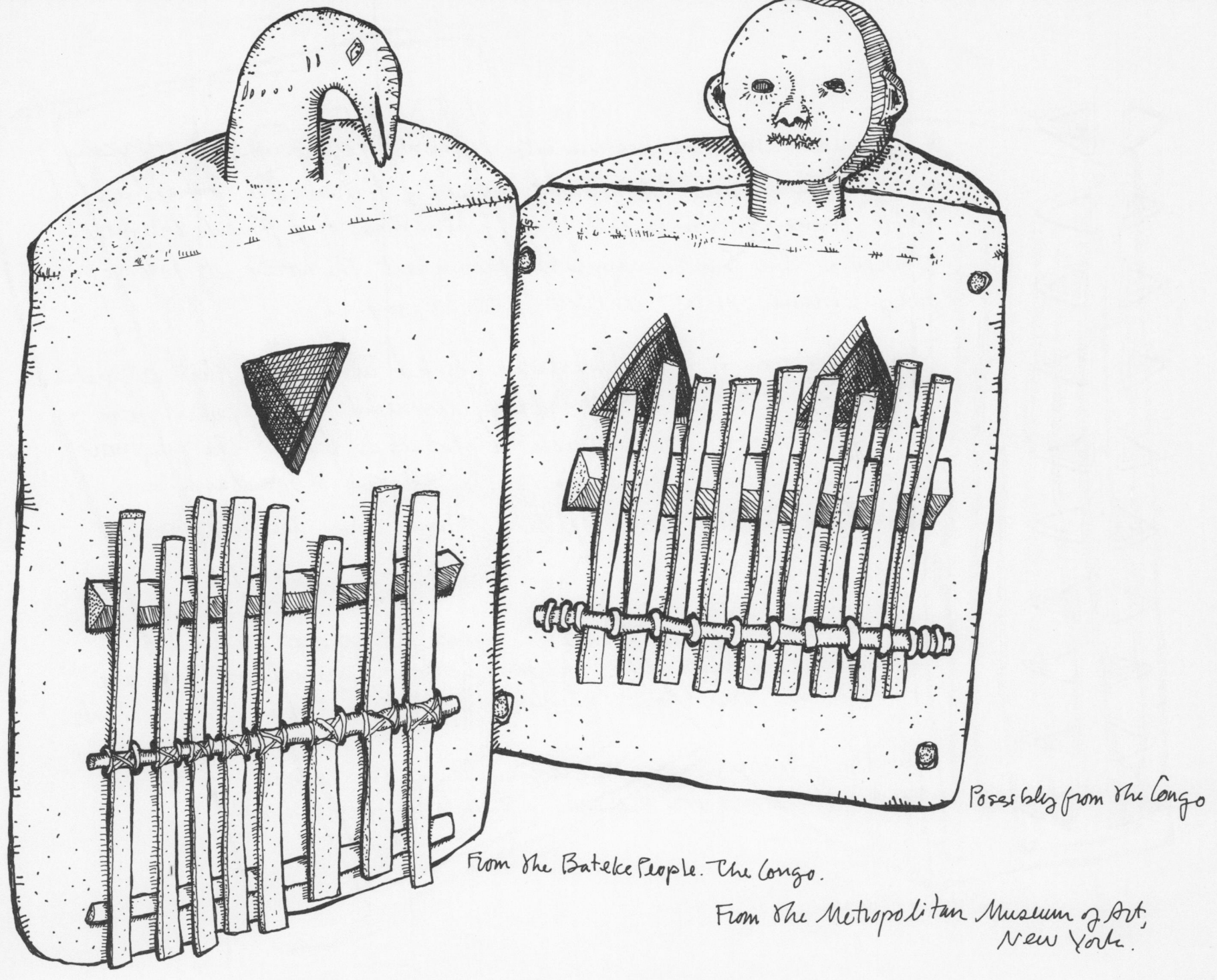

Possibly from the Congo

From the Bateke People. The Congo.

From the Metropolitan Museum of Art,
New York.

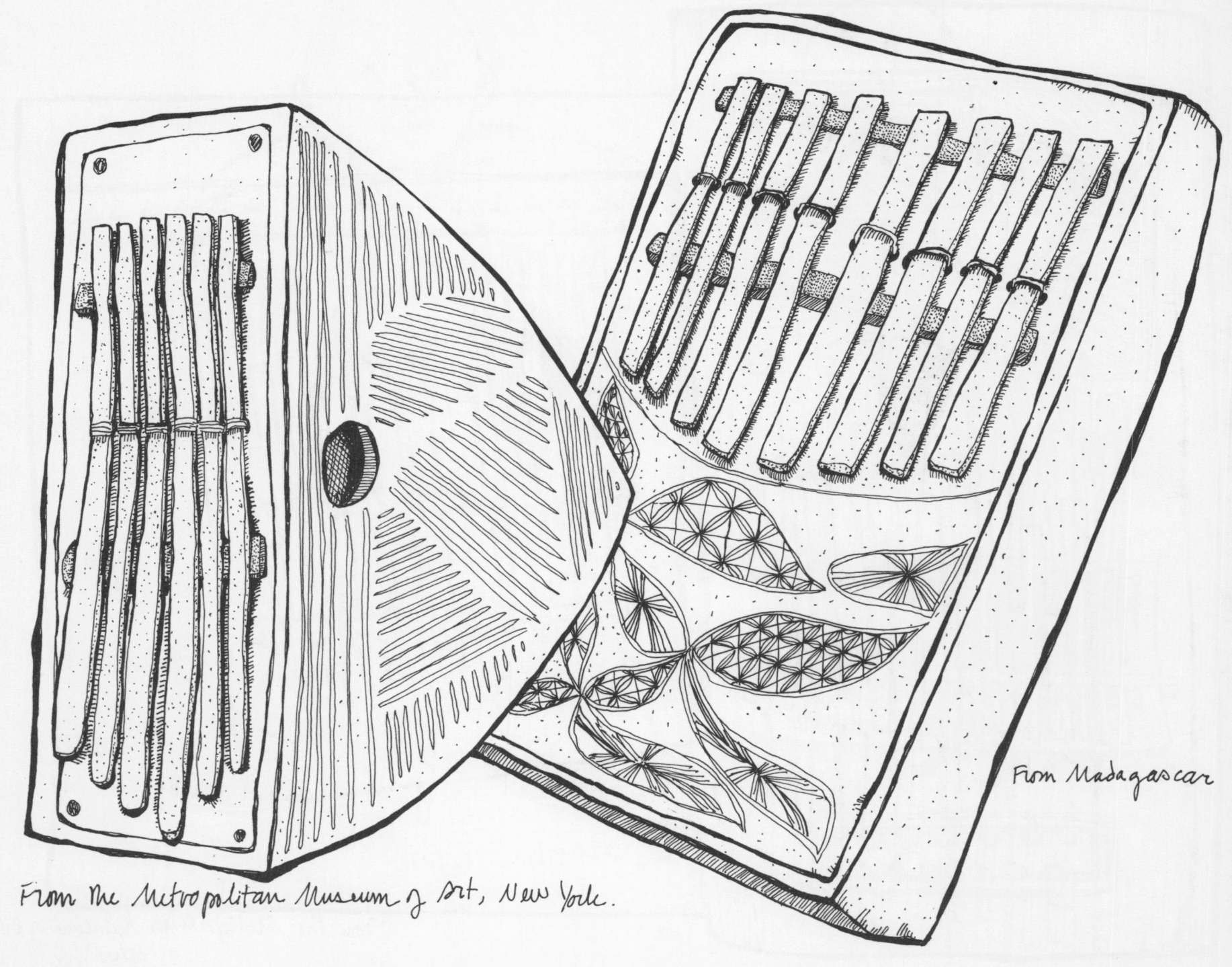

From the Metropolitan Museum of Art, New York.

From Madagascar

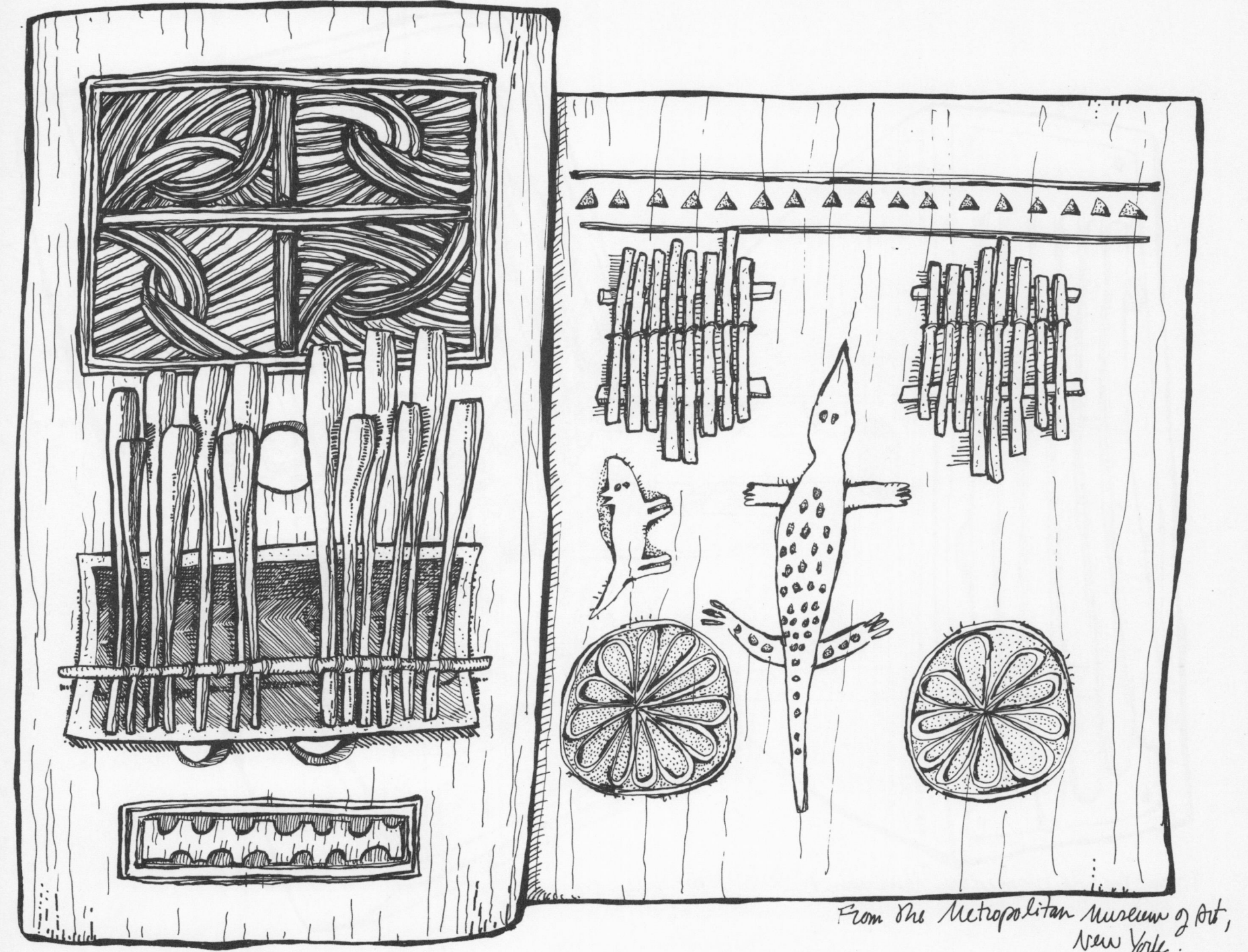

From the Metropolitan Museum of Art, New York.

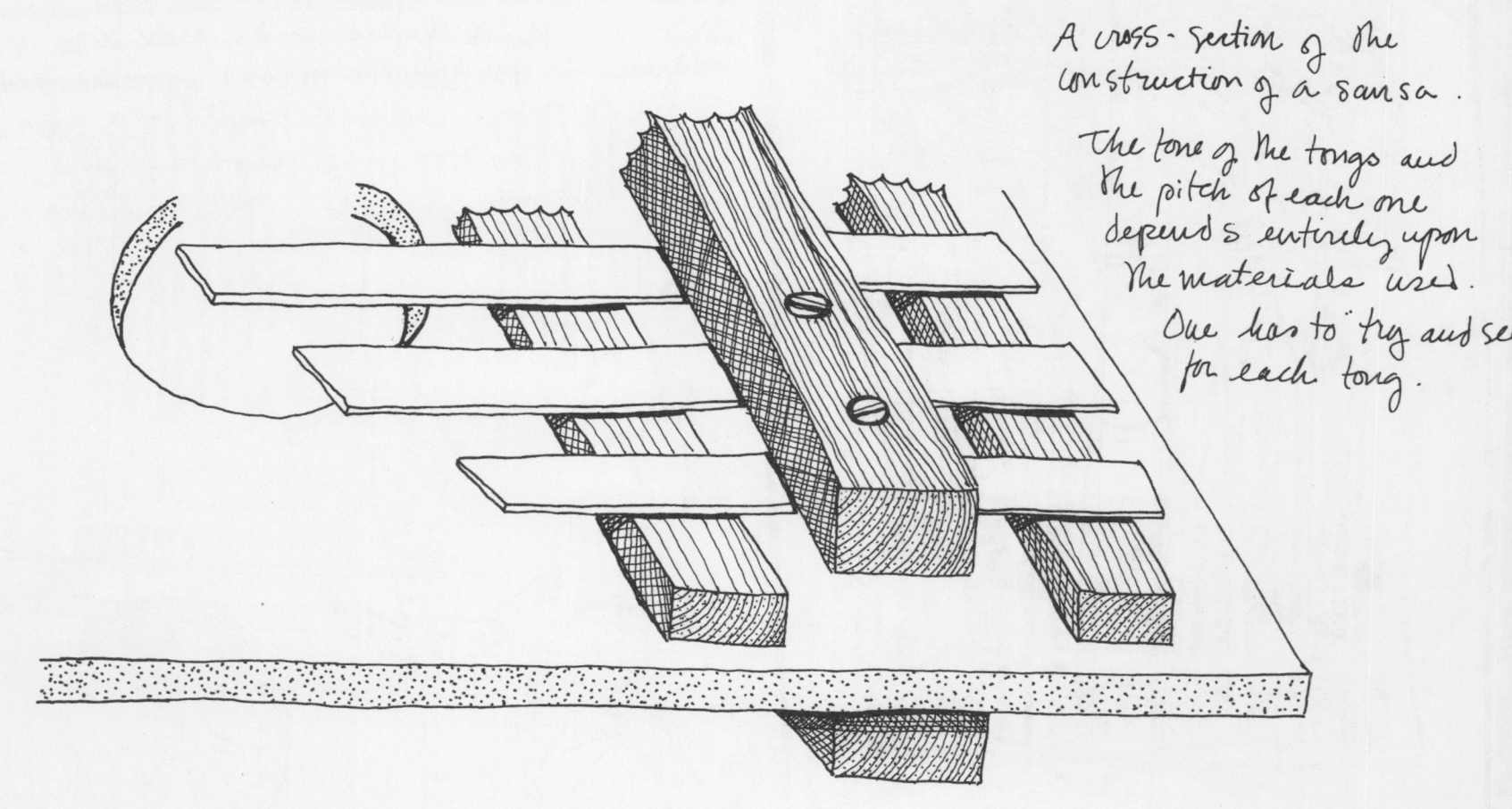

A cross-section of the
construction of a sansa.

The tone of the tongs and
the pitch of each one
depends entirely upon
the materials used.

One has to "try and see"
for each tong.

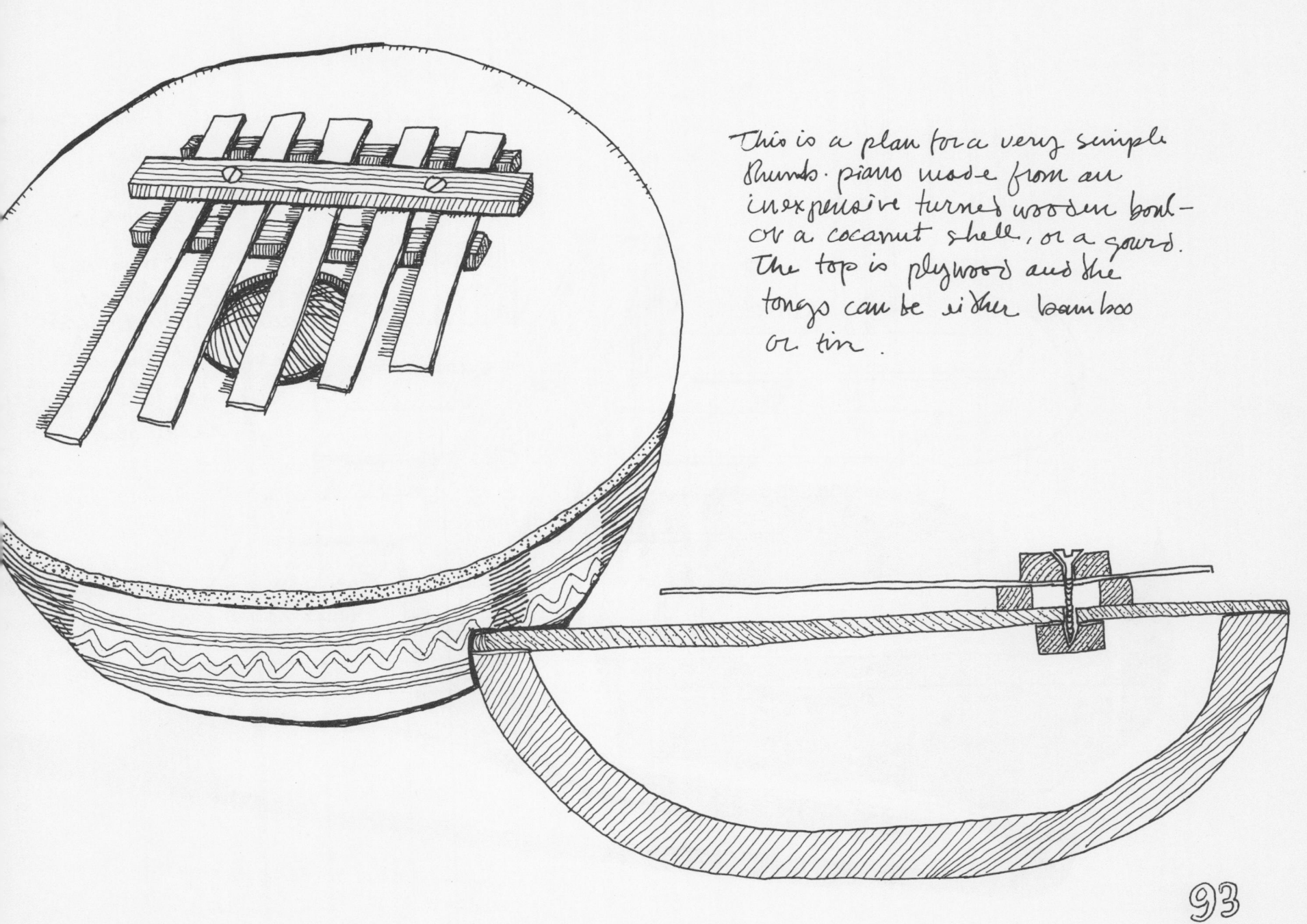

This is a plan for a very simple thumb-piano made from an inexpensive turned wooden bowl — or a coconut shell, or a gourd. The top is plywood and the tongs can be either bamboo or tin.

93

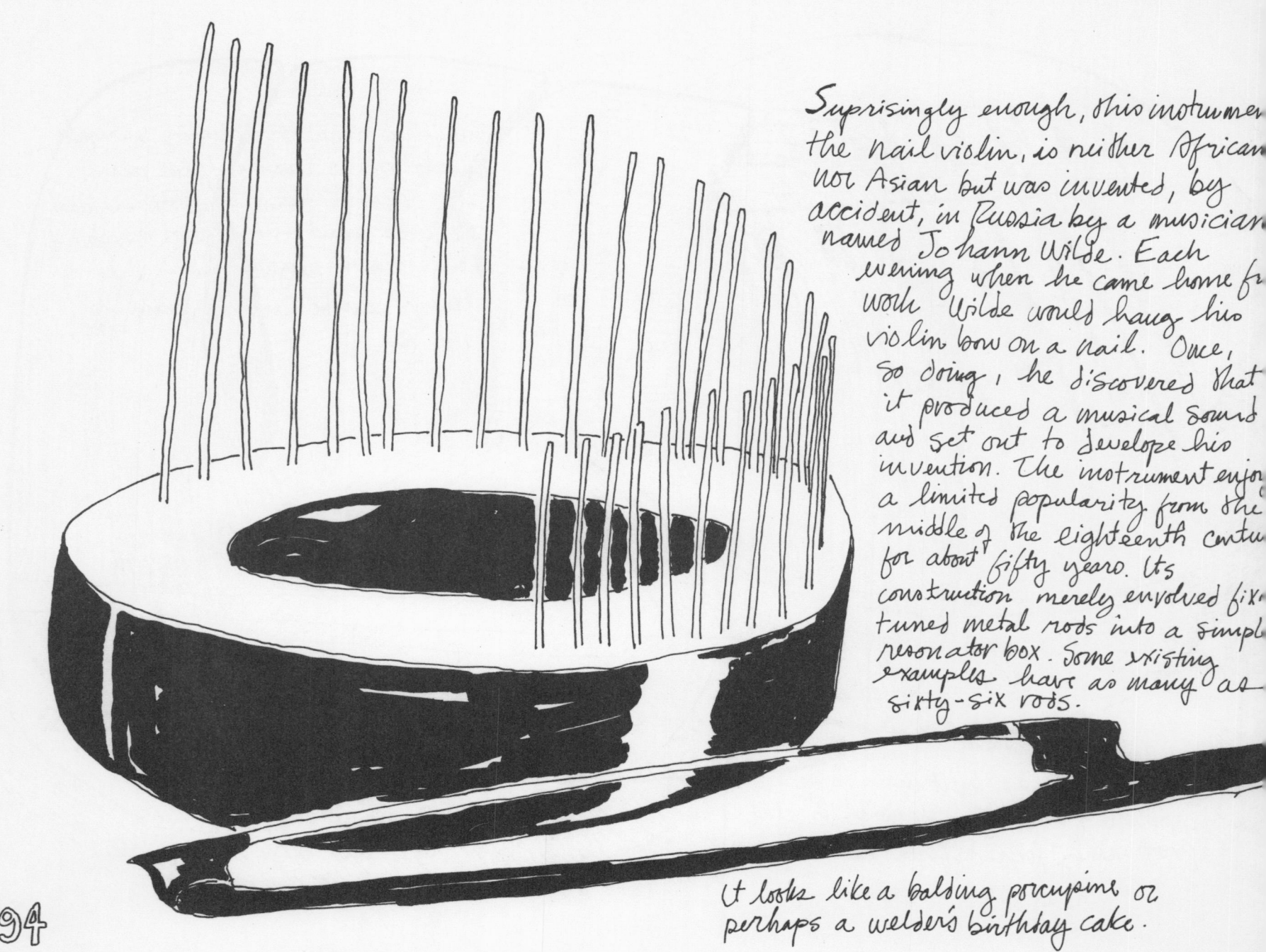

Suprisingly enough, this instrument, the nail violin, is neither African nor Asian but was invented, by accident, in Russia by a musician named Johann Wilde. Each evening when he came home from work Wilde would hang his violin bow on a nail. Once, so doing, he discovered that it produced a musical sound and set out to develope his invention. The instrument enjoyed a limited popularity from the middle of the eighteenth century for about fifty years. Its construction merely envolved fixing tuned metal rods into a simple resonator box. Some existing examples have as many as sixty-six rods.

It looks like a balding porcupine or perhaps a welder's birthday cake.

94

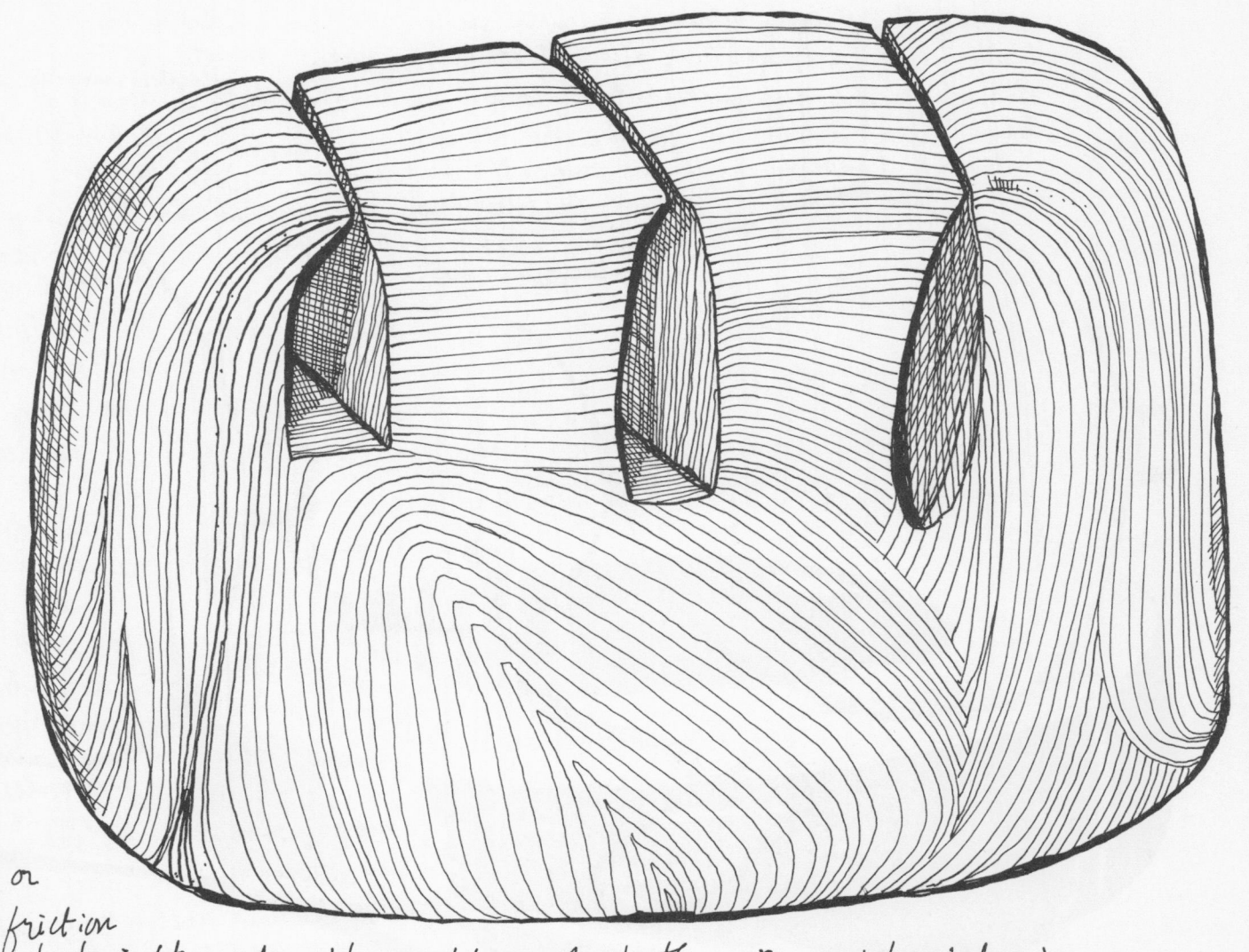

The Kulep Ganeg or
the Nunut is a friction
idiophone from New Ireland. It is played by rubbing the teeth with moistened hands
producing four different tones.   From the Metropolitan Museum of Art, New York.

95

The Kani Niu works like a top. The end sections are attached securely to the axis while the center section, the part held in the hand, has openings that allow it to move freely. A string is attached to the axis which also comes through a hole in the hand-held section. With the other hand the string is pulled and released. Pebbles inside the two outer-most sections produce. By control of the momentum, the rhythm can be maintained or altered at the players' choice.

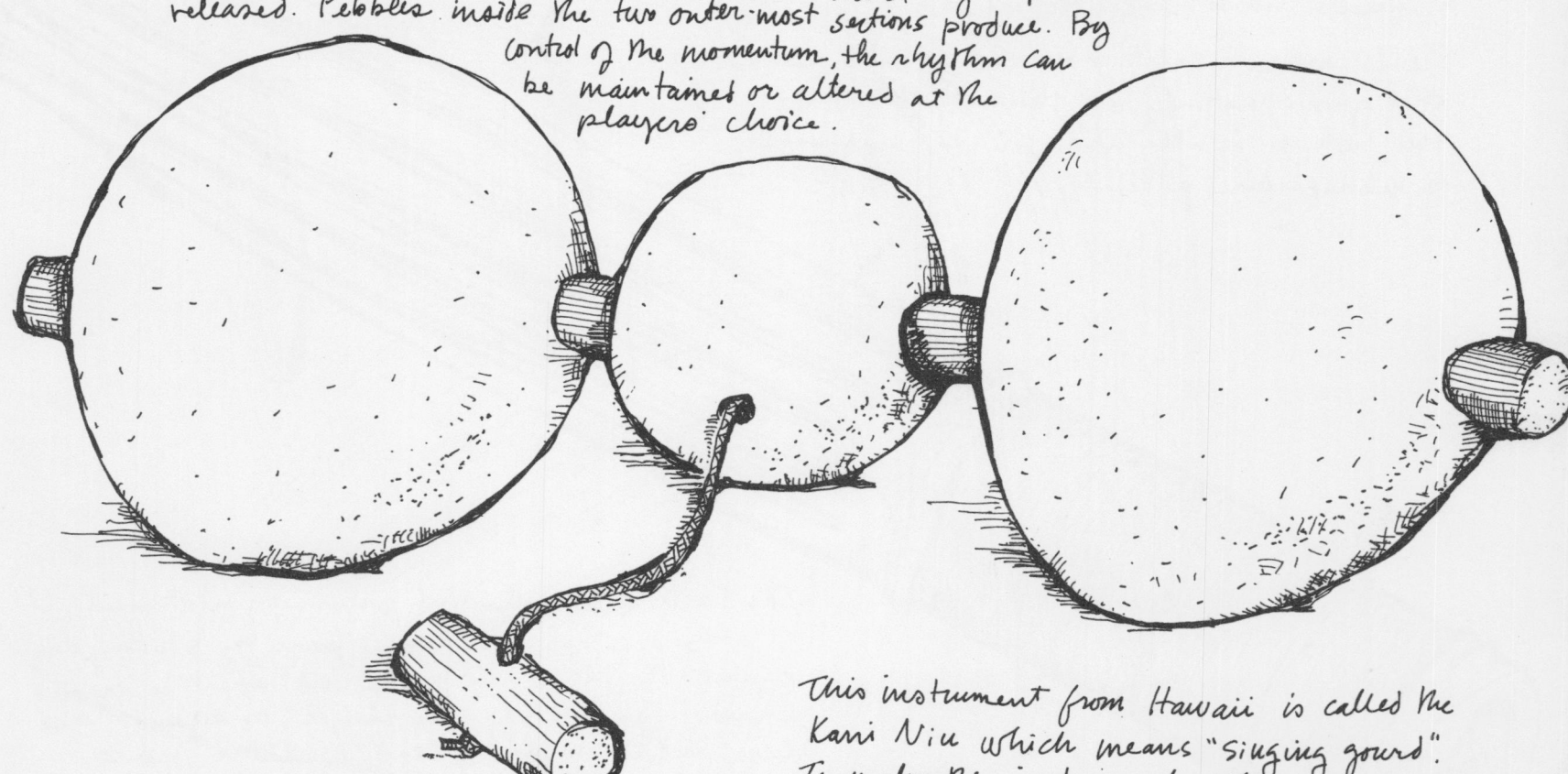

This instrument from Hawaii is called the Kani Niu which means "singing gourd". To make this instrument either gourds or cocanut shells may be used or even a combination of the two. Though size and thickness varies, cocanut shells tend to produce a deeper tone.

This instrument is made of a piece of bamboo split from one joint to another to form forks and wrapped at the next lowest section with fibre for a handle. It is from Hawaii and its name, Puili, means "split bamboo". There is a tree that grows natively in Hawaii, the Hau tree, which is also used for the materials to manufacture a Puili.

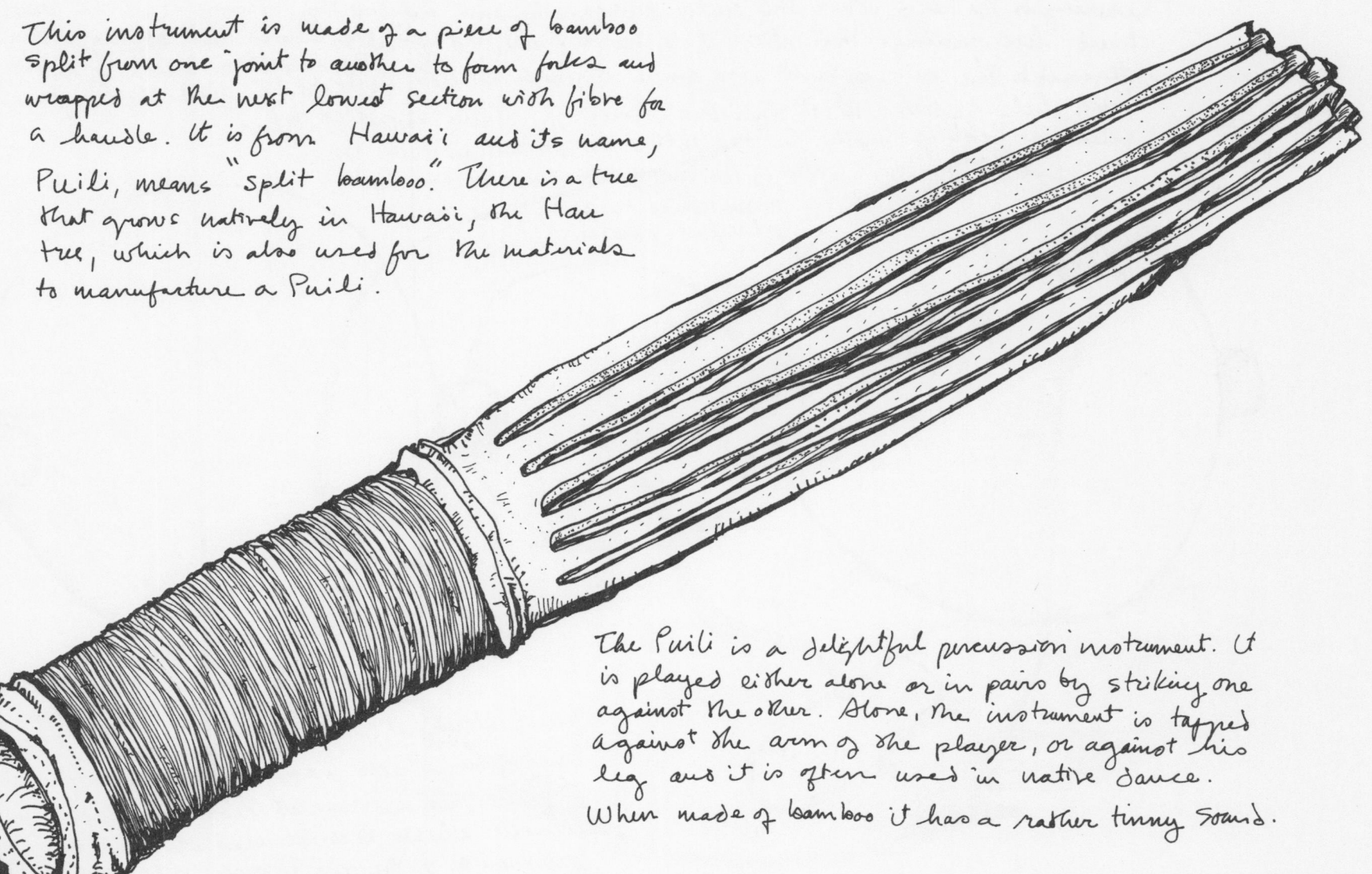

The Puili is a delightful percussion instrument. It is played either alone or in pairs by striking one against the other. Alone, the instrument is tapped against the arm of the player, or against his leg and it is often used in native dance. When made of bamboo it has a rather tinny sound.

The Upu is a Hawaiian drum-like instrument, open at the mouth. It is played by holding it at the mouth with one hand and tapping either on the side or bottom - depending on the tone - or alternately, with the fingers of the other hand.

Upu means "bowl" in Hawaiian.

To make an Upu, simply cut off the longest part of the neck of a gourd and clean out the insides. Shellac or paint at will.

98

Believe it or not, this musical instrument neither flies nor chirps. It is, you might say, a rather well-dressed maraca. To construct an Uli Uli, which is a native Hawaiian instrument, select a gourd about 14" in diameter. Remove the neck and replace the seeds with pebbles. In place of the neck, attach a dowel providing a handle about 6" long. At the end of the handle opposite the gourd attach a light plywood or heavy cardboard disc about 10" in diameter. Decorate this with feathers. The Uli Uli is used in native dances and is often played in pairs. To play it, reach under the feathers, grasp the handle and play like maracas.

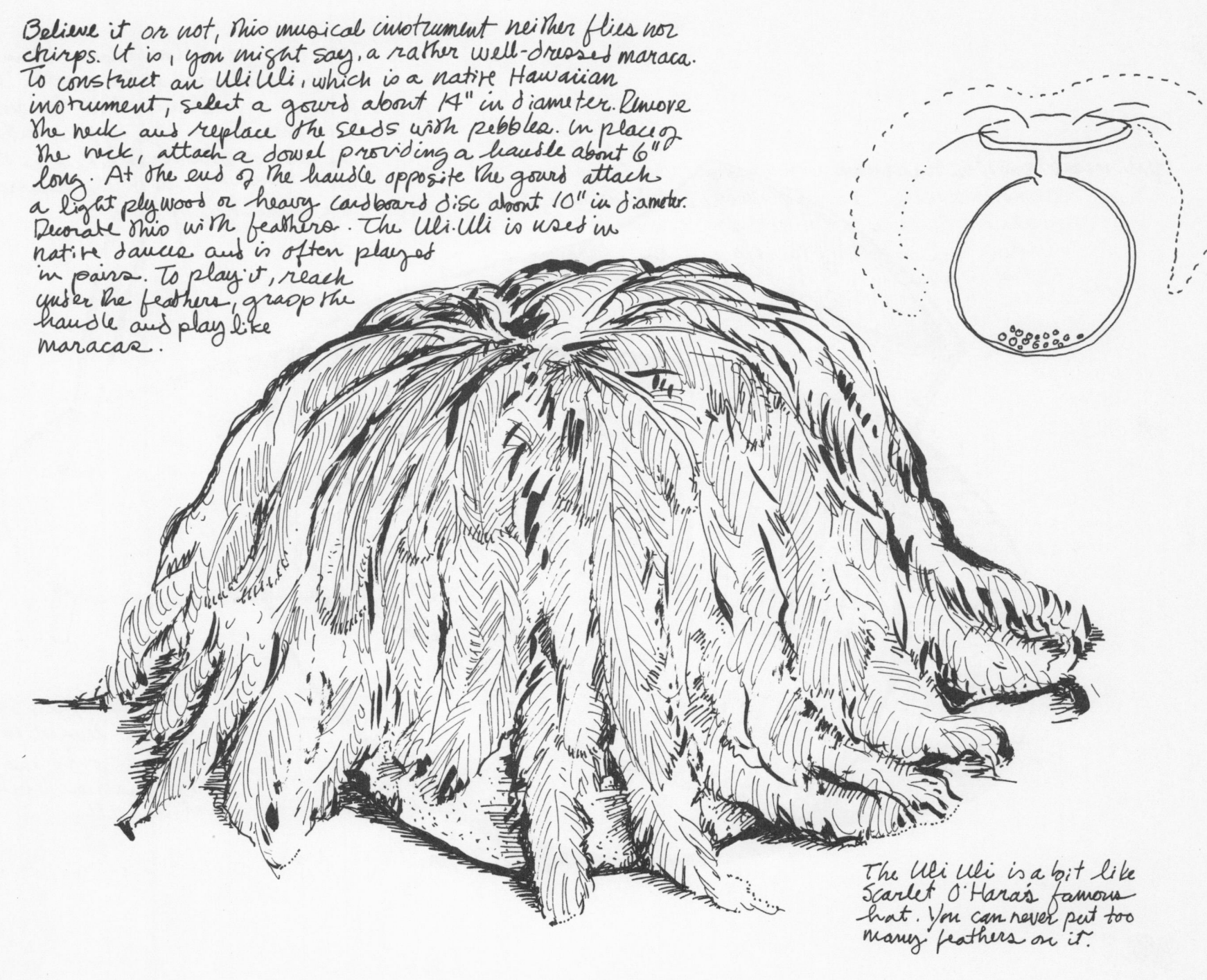

The Uli Uli is a bit like Scarlet O'Hara's famous hat. You can never put too many feathers on it.

This scraper, made of gourd, is from Cuba.
Gourd is easily carved or incised and instruments,
such as this one, are obviously simple to
make. The appeal of this one is in the pattern
of the grooves.

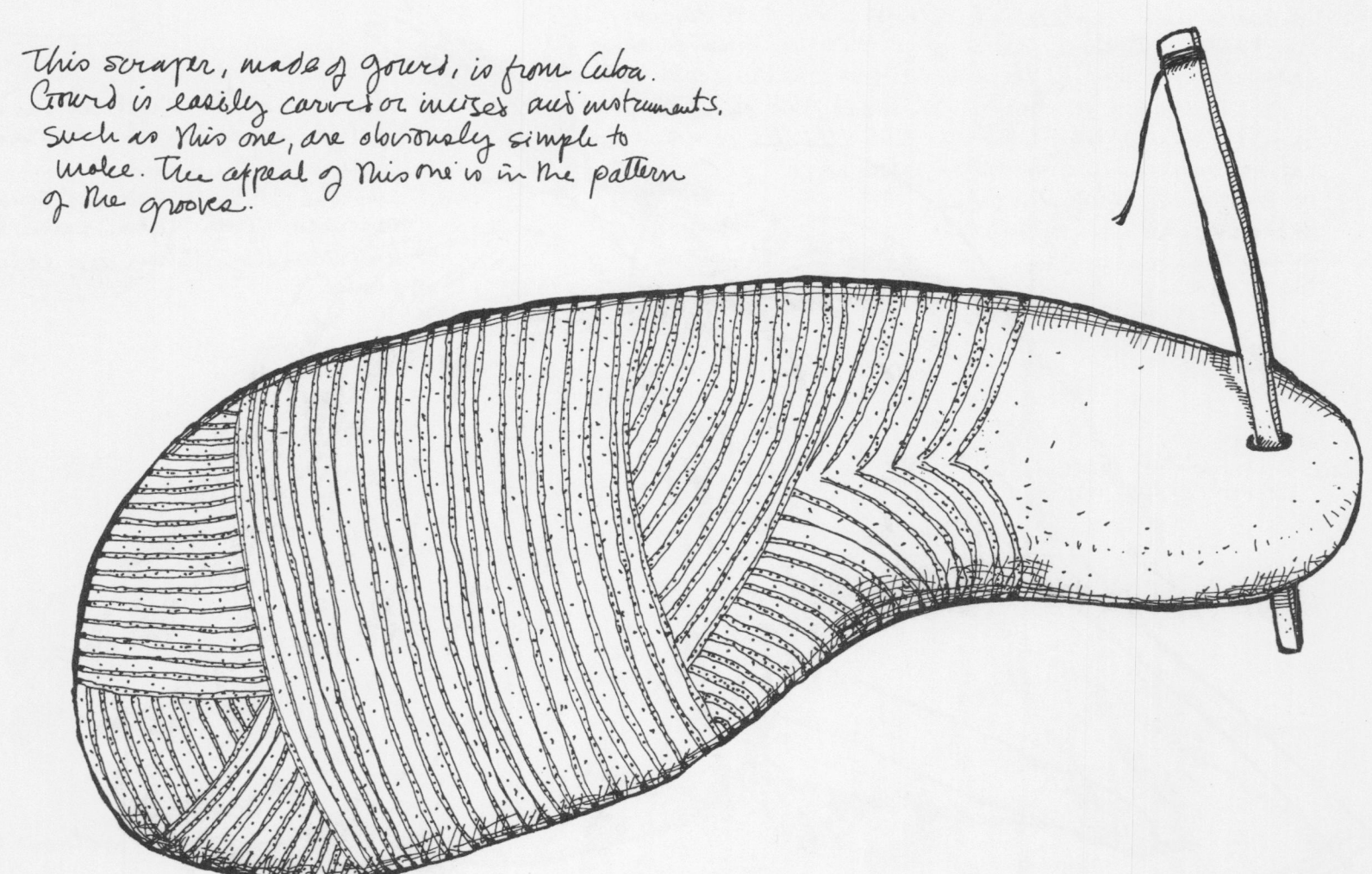

From the Metropolitan Museum of Art, New York.

100

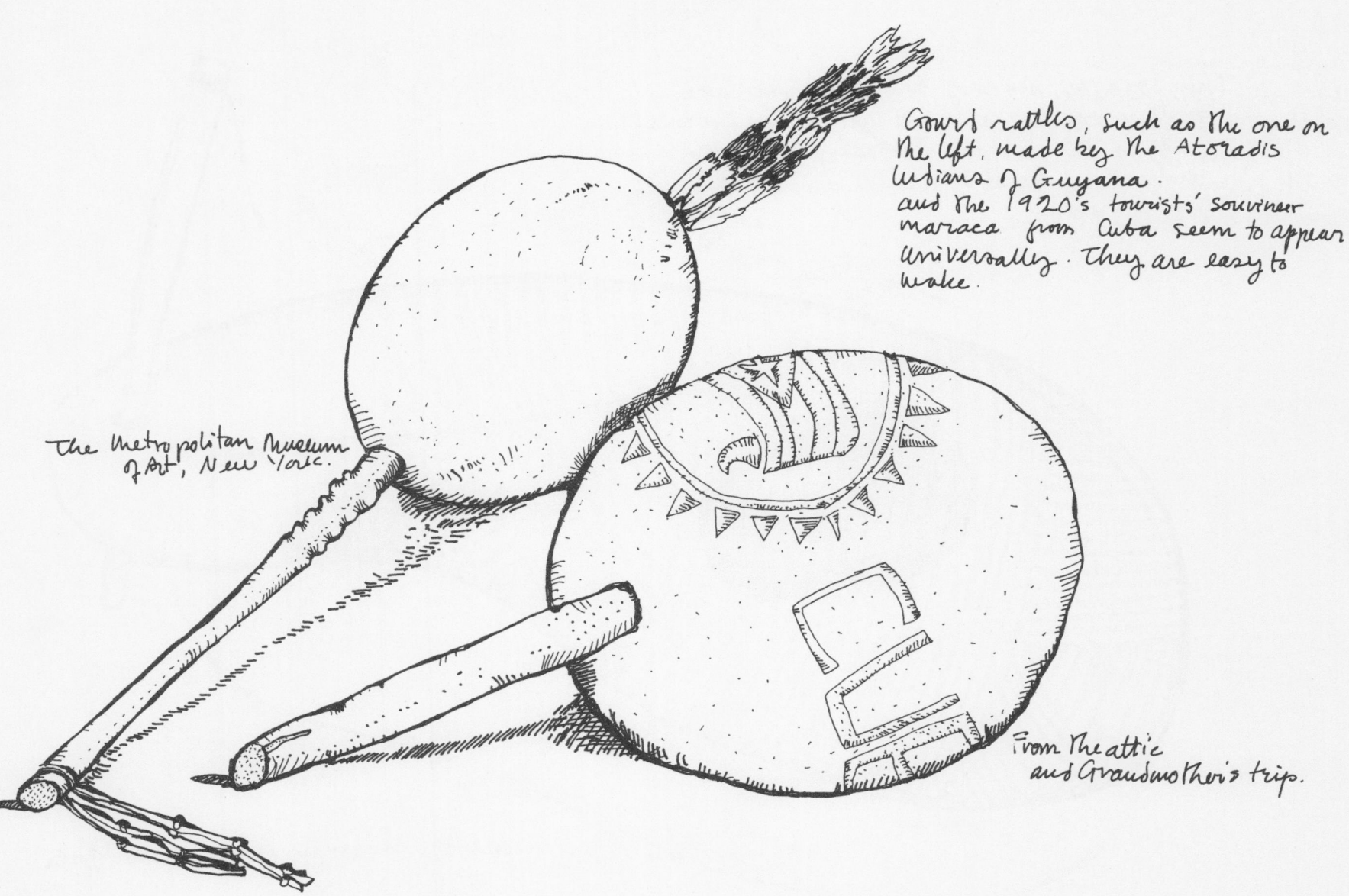

Gourd rattles, such as the one on
the left, made by the Atoradis
Indians of Guyana.
and the 1920's tourists' souvineer
maraca from Cuba seem to appear
universally. They are easy to
make.

The Metropolitan Museum
of Art, New York.

From the attic
and Grandmother's trip.

101

This is a scraper and gourd
resonator for playing a
notched stick. The stick
is held over the opening
in the gourd.
Hopi Indian. Northern Arizona.

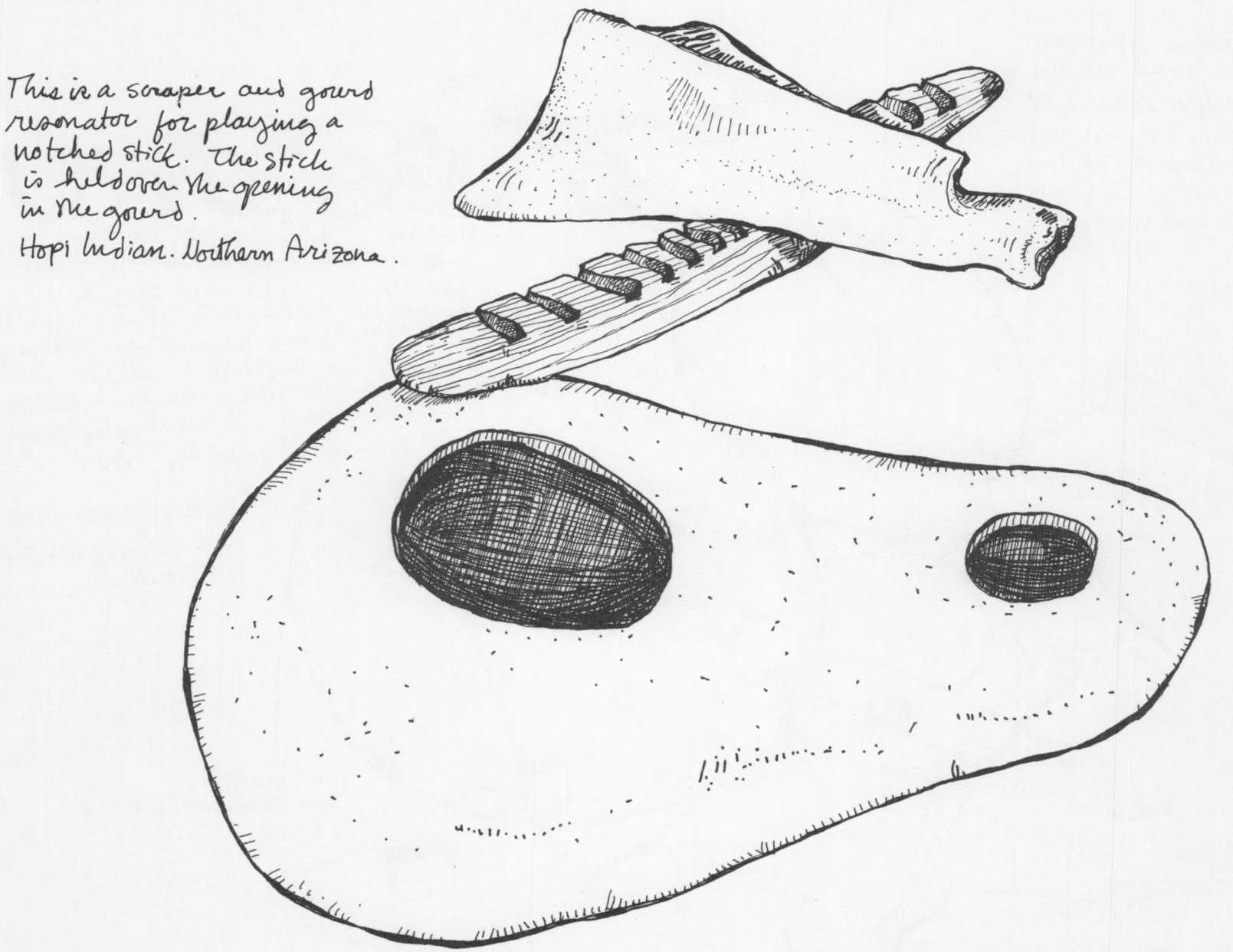

102

From the Metropolitan Museum of Art, New York.

The American composer,
Harry Partch, would not like to
think of himself as a musical
instrument builder or inventor
yet his instruments, in their
imaginative use of ordinary
and unusual materials,
speak for themselves.

this instrument called
the Gourd Tree and Cone Gongs
is made of twelve Chinese
temple bells attached to gourds
and then to a eucalyptus bough
with 3/16" rods.

The cone gongs were
nose cones of airplane
gas tanks.

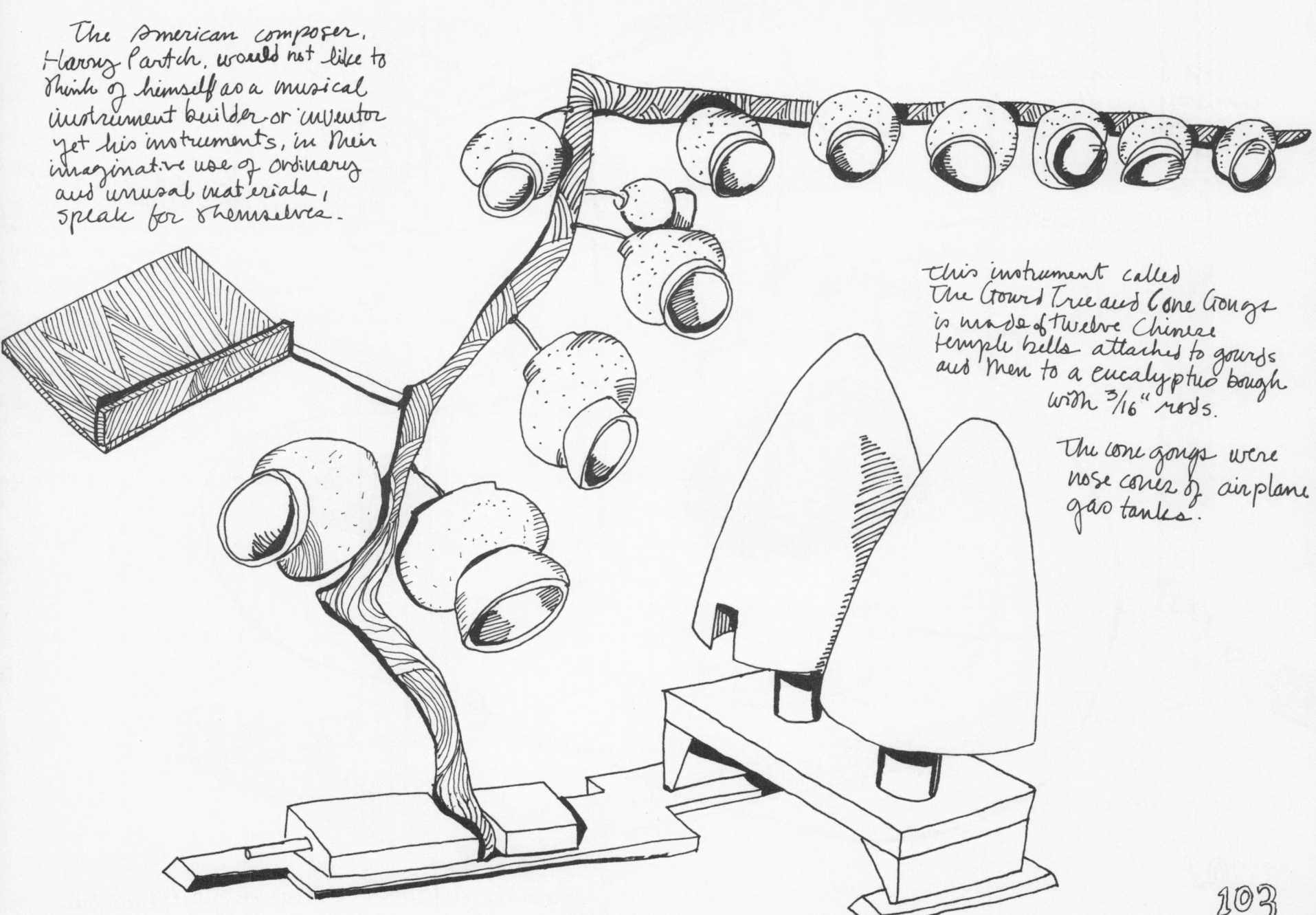

103

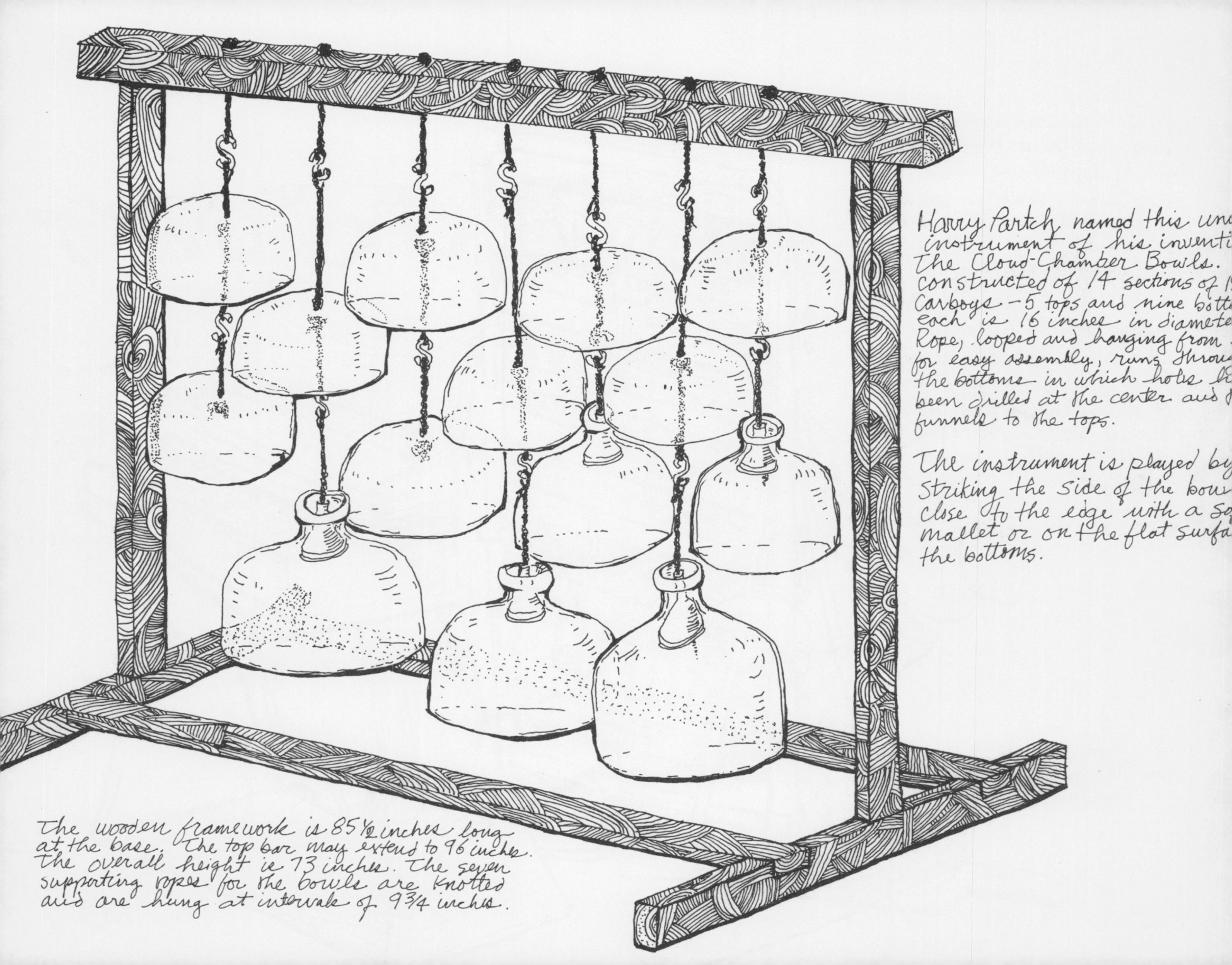

Harry Partch named this und
instrument of his inventi
The Cloud-Chamber Bowls.
constructed of 14 sections of 1'
Carboys – 5 tops and nine botte
each is 16 inches in diamete
Rope, looped and hanging from
for easy assembly, runs throug
the bottoms in which holes h
been drilled at the center and
funnels to the tops.

The instrument is played by
striking the side of the bow
close to the edge with a so
mallet or on the flat surfa
the bottoms.

The wooden framework is 85½ inches long
at the base. The top bar may extend to 96 inches.
The overall height is 73 inches. The seven
supporting ropes for the bowls are knotted
and are hung at intervals of 9¾ inches.

The curious-looking
instrument operates on
the principle of door-bell
chimes, tuned and attached
to a key-board mechanism.
It was used in an American
circus and is called
the Una-Fon.

From the Circus World Museum.
Baraboo, Wisconsin.

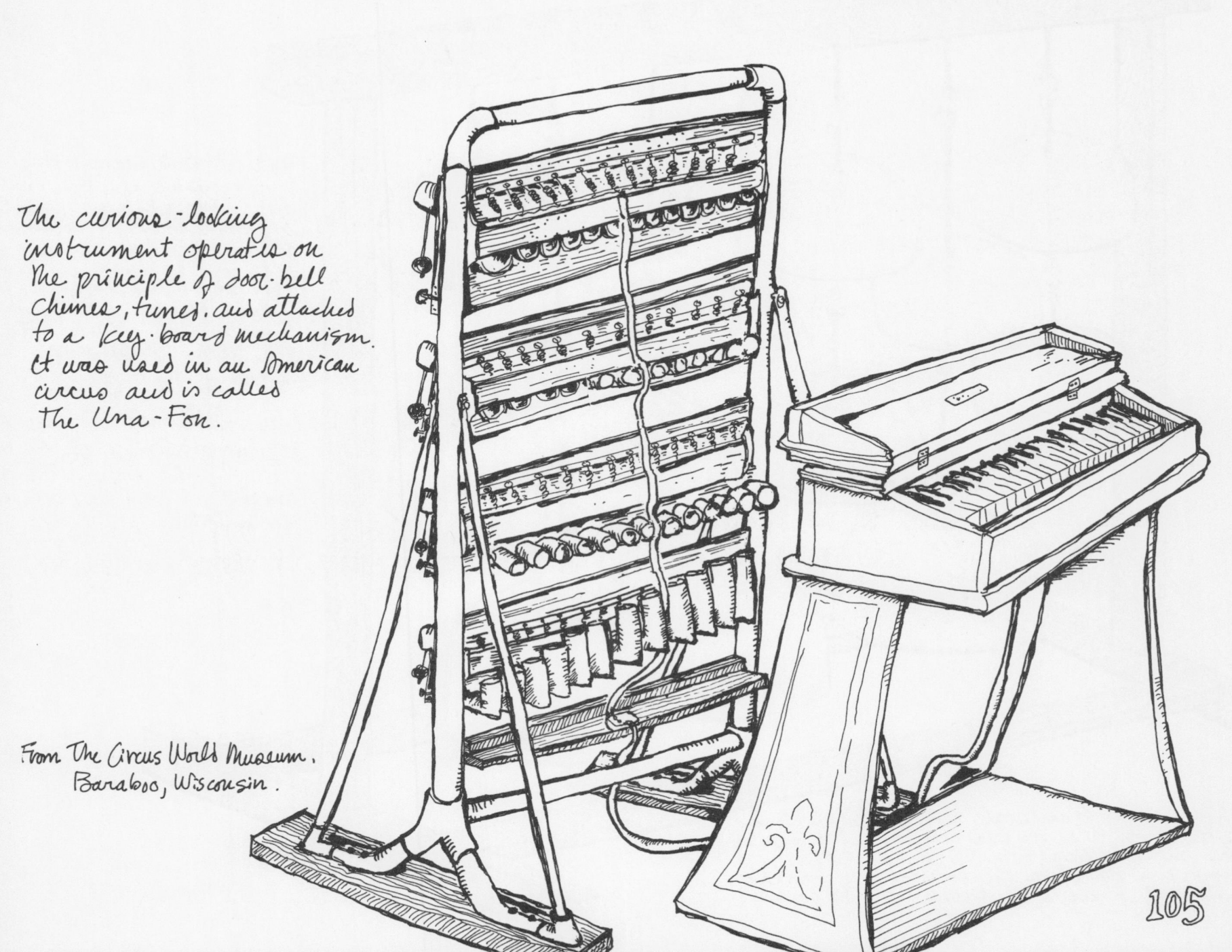

105

Probably the first musical instrument that man discovered was the human body's potential to accompany itself: clapping hands, foot-patting, while singing or whistling. Or just for the delight of the sound any one of those makes.

Tap dancing, a tradition as American as apple pie, is the obvious developement of that instinct with the addition of two distinct influences; the barefoot dance of Black Africa brought to America by slaves, and clog dancing with wood-soled shoes of European emigrants. Added to that were steel taps of vaudeville invention. Combined, tap dancing represnts both a dance form and a musical instrument.

In America the traditions met, as they have in so many ways, and they have formed something entirely new, entirely unique, yet something almost as old as music.

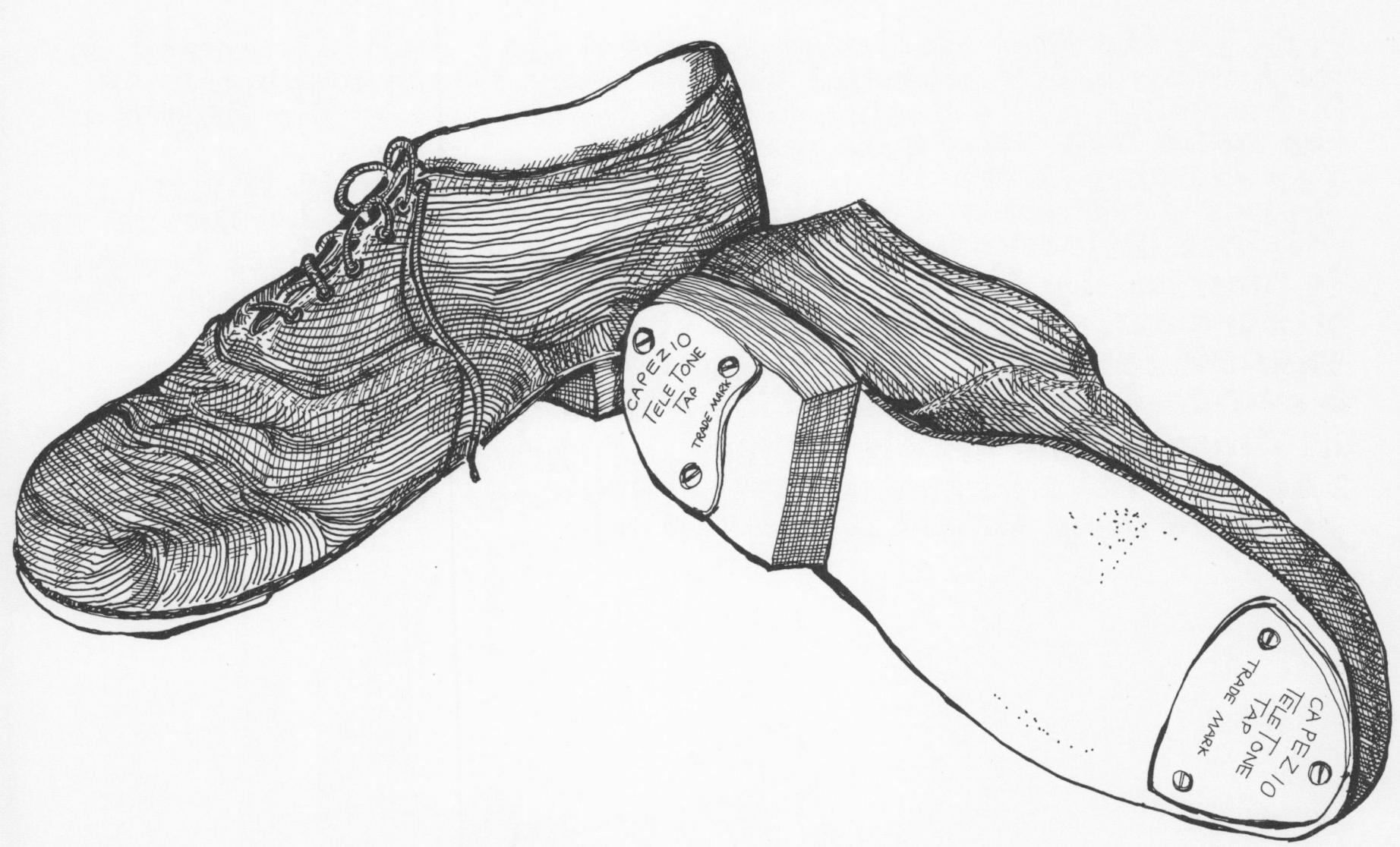

Acknowledgements

A wise man once said that a writer of a first book ought to acknowledge anyone for any reason he chooses. The reason being, I suppose, that there may never be the opportunity again. On the other hand, there is the chance that if he acknowledges enough people well enough he may well be given another chance, perhaps writing a telephone book.

There are some people who must be acknowledged for without them, each in a different way, this book would have been impossible. I begin, as we all did, with parents. Had mine gotten anything but the delineator they got, an oboist or flutist or banjo-builder, perhaps he would have written a book about art. They deserve much thanks.

Louise and Lady Jane, my best critics from the start, have taught me how to learn for myself.

Ginni (and Ezra who started talking while this book was being written but still cannot say calliope) taught me a lot about birth and growth.

Elizabeth taught me to use the first pen I drew with.

Bill Ballantine taught me much about using two pens by his example which I hold in high regard.

Laurence Gadd, my publisher and friend, has the patience of Job. I thank him.

Brendan Gill, with a glass of wine and a good story — NEVER about musical instruments, was a great help when I was getting cross-eyed with research.

And Eugenia ... for her wonderful self.

And Ellen.

109

Much of the work of drawing instruments for this book was accomplished at the Metropolitan Museum of Art, New York. I have given credit throughout the book when instruments appear from that collection and a special acknowledgement is due for that vast resource and permission to draw upon it. Some of the instruments were on loan to the Goddard-Riverside Community Center, New York and I am thankful for the help and co-operation of Alexandra Padua while I worked on portions of this book there. I am grateful to the generous help and criticism and direction of Guilliano Chicco.

Acknowledgement is due with special thanks to The American Museum of Natural History to do drawing of the pluriare on p.13 and to the Eakins Press, New York for the poem from Willard Trask's Classical Black African Poems.

I wish to thank the Oxford University Press for permission to quote from The Concise Oxford Dictionary, and the Viking Press for Carl van Doren's transcription of the Benjamin Franklin letter in van Doren's Benjamin Franklin's Autobiographical Writings. Also Da Capo Press, New York, for the information on the Harry Partch instruments. And the Circus World Museum Library, Baraboo, Wisconsin for the Una-Fon.

Special appreciation and acknowledgement is due Pete Seeger for a life-time of work in American folk music. I am especially grateful for his work with Kim Loy Wong on the steel drum.

Also for John Putnam and his work on the Appalachian dulcimer.

I wish to thank the Council of the Southern Mountains in Clintwood, Virginia and in Berea, Kentucky.

I am grateful to Padraic O coilean of the Irish Consulate in New York and to John Ryan and Comhaltas Ceoltoiri Eireann for information on the Bodhran.

And to The Yeshiva University Cantorial Training Institute and to Cantor Nulman for information on the Shofar.

Also to Johnny Pineapple for his information on native Hawaiian instruments.

Capezio Ballet Makers were generous with information on tap dancing.

110

SOURCES

OF ADDITIONAL INFORMATION FOR MAKERS OF THEIR OWN MUSICAL INSTRUMENTS

The following is a list of some sources that may be helpful for an amateur instrument maker. If the information is not readily available in libraries or book-stores orders can generally be addressed directly to the publishers.

BANJO-BUILDING

Earl Scruggs and The Five String Banjo
Peer International Corp.
1619 Broadway
New York, N.Y. 10019

How to Make a Banjo and a Guitar-Banjo
by Fuss Stamm
printed privately and available through
organizations such as Mugwamps (p. 114)
with plans, diagrams, and blue-prints

MUSICAL BOWS

The Buffy Sainte-Marie Song Book
Grosset & Dunlap.
51 Madison Avenue
New York, N.Y. 10010

DULCIMER MAKING

In Search of The Wild Dulcimer
by Robert Force and Albert d'Ossché
Vintage Books
201 E. 50th Street
New York, N.Y. 10022

The Dulcimer Book
by John Pearse
Rosetti and Co. Ltd.
138 Old Street
London, EC1 U.K.

The Plucked Dulcimer
by John Putnam
1905 Hopefield Road
Silver Springs, Md. 20904

CONTINUED

MORE DULCIMERS

The Dulcimer Book
and
The Dulcimer People
by Jean Richie
Oak Publications
33 W. 60th Street
New York, N.Y. 10023

GUITARS

I did not deal at all with
guitar construction but there
are two good books on the
subject I cannot fail to
mention.

Guitar Construction from A to Z
available through The Society of the Classical Guitar
409 E. 50th Street
New York, N.Y. 10022
°°°
The Guitar Book
A Handbook for Electric and Acoustic Guitars
Harper and Row
10 E. 53rd Street
New York, N.Y. 10022

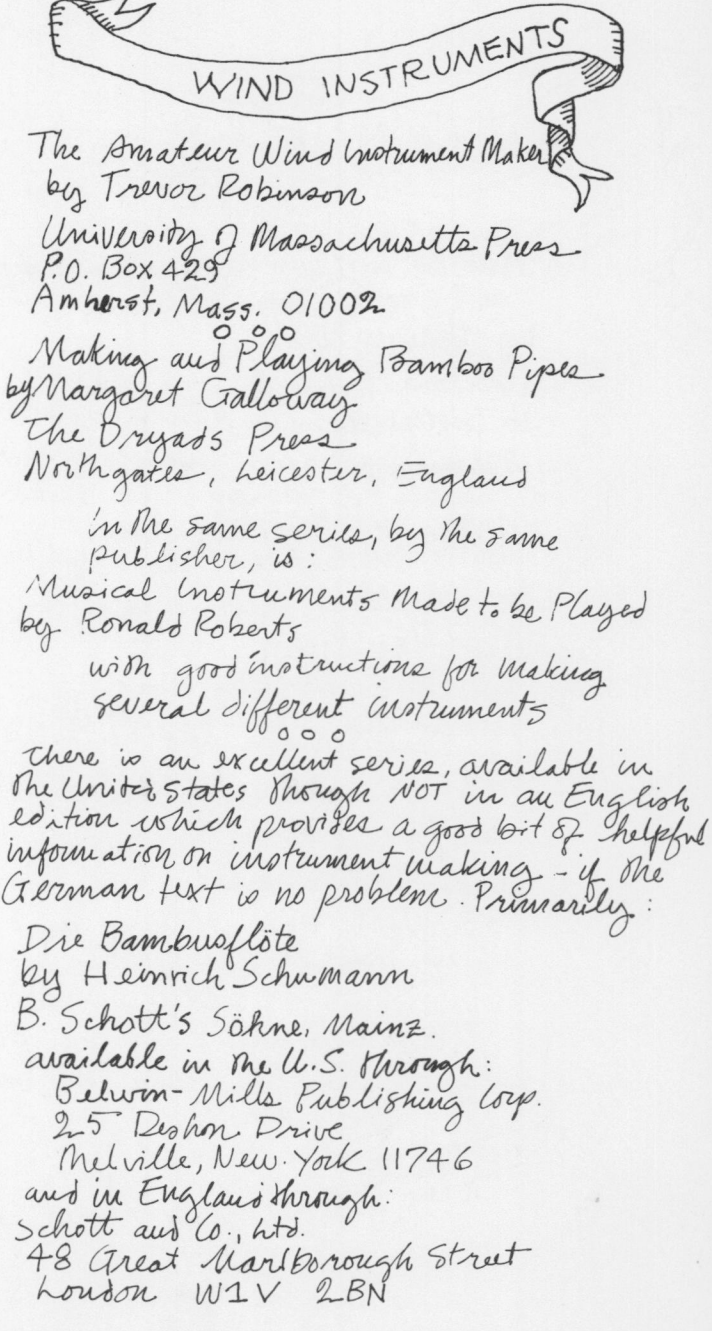

WIND INSTRUMENTS

The Amateur Wind Instrument Maker
by Trevor Robinson
University of Massachusetts Press
P.O. Box 429
Amherst, Mass. 01002
°°°
Making and Playing Bamboo Pipes
by Margaret Galloway
The Dryads Press
Northgates, Leicester, England

in the same series, by the same
publisher, is:
Musical Instruments Made to be Played
by Ronald Roberts
with good instructions for making
several different instruments
°°°
there is an excellent series, available in
the United States though NOT in an English
edition which provides a good bit of helpful
information on instrument making - if the
German text is no problem. Primarily:

Die Bambusflöte
by Heinrich Schumann
B. Schott's Söhne, Mainz.
available in the U.S. through:
   Belwin-Mills Publishing Corp.
   25 Deshon Drive
   Melville, New York 11746
and in England through:
Schott and Co., Ltd.
48 Great Marlborough Street
London W1V 2BN

WITHDRAWN